James Gilchrist Swan

The Indians of Cape Flattery

At the Entrance to the Strait of Fuca, Washington Territory

James Gilchrist Swan

The Indians of Cape Flattery
At the Entrance to the Strait of Fuca, Washington Territory

ISBN/EAN: 9783744677547

Printed in Europe, USA, Canada, Australia, Japan

Cover: Foto ©Suzi / pixelio.de

More available books at **www.hansebooks.com**

SMITHSONIAN CONTRIBUTIONS TO KNOWLEDGE.

220

THE

INDIANS OF CAPE FLATTERY,

AT THE ENTRANCE TO THE STRAIT OF FUCA,
WASHINGTON TERRITORY.

BY

JAMES G. SWAN.

[ACCEPTED FOR PUBLICATION, JUNE 1868.]

COMMISSION
TO WHICH THIS PAPER HAS BEEN REFERRED.

GEORGE GIBBS.
JEFFRIES WYMAN.

JOSEPH HENRY,
Secretary S. I.

ADVERTISEMENT.

The following memoir on the Makah Indians was prepared at the request of the Smithsonian Institution by Mr. James G. Swan, who, for several years, resided among them in the capacity of teacher and dispenser of medicines under the Government of the United States. Mr. Swan had previously become well acquainted with the Indian tribes of the Pacific, and had published a small work detailing his adventures among them. In 1855 he accompanied the late Maj. Gen. Stevens, then Governor of Washington Territory, while making treaties with the Makahs and other tribes, and was subsequently appointed to the position above mentioned.

For the information of those not acquainted with the relation of the United States to the Indian tribes it may be remarked that where lands occupied by them are required for settlement, or where their proximity to the whites is found inexpedient, it has been the practice to extinguish their possessory rights by treaty, paying them generally in annuities of money or goods, and setting apart a portion of land, sometimes within their original territory, in other cases at a distance, for their exclusive occupation, upon which no white settlers are allowed to intrude. These tracts are known as reservations, and are under charge of government "agents," often assisted by teachers, mechanics, &c.

In the absence of Mr. Swan, the editorial supervision of the work was committed to Mr. George Gibbs, who has added a few notes.

JOSEPH HENRY,
Secretary S. I.

SMITHSONIAN INSTITUTION,
1869.

PREFATORY NOTE.

THE philological family, to which the Makahs belong, is that known on old maps as the "Wakash Nation," a name given by Captain Cook from the word of greeting used by the Indians of King George's, or Nootka Sound, where he first met them. For the purpose of classification it may be convenient to preserve the name of Nootka, which has been usually recognized, as that of the language in general, although it originally sprung from an equally trivial source. It is to be observed that there are no *nations* in our sense of the word among these Indians, but those speaking even the same dialect of a common language are often broken up into separate bands under different chiefs, and their various appellations belong only to localities. Occasionally a chief, more powerful and sagacious than the rest, will bring several of these under his control, but his power is after all limited, and dies with him.

The territory occupied by this NOOTKA family is not as yet clearly defined on the north. Generally speaking, it embraces, besides that of the Makahs, on the south side of the Strait of Fuca, described by Mr. Swan in the following paper, Vancouver Island, with the exception of a small part of its northeastern border, occupied by intrusive bands of the Hailtsa, and the southwestern portion extending from Sooke Harbor to above Komooks in the Gulf of Georgia, which is held by tribes of the Shchwapmukh or Sélish family. It also covers part of the adjacent continent on the Gulf of Georgia and Johnston's Straits, being thus enclosed by Sélish tribes on the south and east and by those of the Hailtsa on the north. The Kwilléyutes on the coast of Washington Territory, south of the Makahs, are a remote branch of the Sélish, and the Clallams lying east along the southern shore of Fuca Strait are another tribe of that family, closely connected with the Sooke and Songhus Indians of the southeastern end of Vancouver Island.

GEORGE GIBBS.

WASHINGTON, January, 1870.

TABLE OF CONTENTS.

	PAGE
Name of the Tribe	1
Geographical Position	1
Character of the Reservation	2
Census of the Tribe	2
Physical Characteristics	3
Dwellings	4
Picture Writing	7
Social Life	10
Festivals	13
Sports of Children	14
Dress	15
Personal Ornaments	17
Care of Children	18
Food, and Method of obtaining it	19
Fishing and Sealing	27
Trade	30
Tools	33
Canoes	35
Whaling and Fishing Gear	39
Boxes, Baskets, Mats, &c.	42
Feather and Dog's-Hair Blankets	43
Gambling Implements	44
Mats, Baskets, Ornaments, &c.	45
Weapons, Bows, Arrows, Fish and Bird Spears	47
Songs	49
Method of Warfare	50
Government	52
History, Traditions, &c.	55
Mythology	61
Winter Ceremonies	62
Legends	64
Masks and Masquerading	69
Shamanistic Ceremonies	73
Shamanism, or Magic and Medicine	76
Diseases	79
Remedies	80
Funeral Ceremonies	85
Superstitions	86
Computation of Time	91
Legend of the South Wind	92
Vocabulary of the Makah Dialect	93
Local Nomenclature of the Makah	105

(vii)

LIST OF ILLUSTRATIONS.

		PAGE
Figure 1.	Thunderbird of the Makahs	9
Figure 2.	Makah Indian in Wet Weather Dress	16
Figure 3.	Headdress and Pendant of Dentalium	16
Figure 4.	Harpoon Point and Line	20
Figure 5.	Sealskin Buoy	20
Figure 6.	Whaling Canoe	21
Figure 7.	Whaling Paddle	21
Figure 8.	Saddle of Whale's Blubber	22
Figure 9.	Halibut Hook	23
Figure 10.	Halibut Chopper	23
Figure 11.	Ladle of "Big-horn"	26
Figure 12.	Spoon of *Aploceras* Horn	26
Figure 13.	Wooden Ladle	27
Figure 15.	Stone Adze	34
Figure 16.	Chisel	34
Figure 17.	Stone Hammer	35
Figure 18.	Canoe, showing Method of Scarphing	37
Figure 19.	Clyoquot Paddle	37
Figure 20.	Canoe under Sail	38
Figure 21.	Codfish Hook	41
Figure 22.	Fish Club	42
Figure 23.	Fish Club	42
Figure 24.	Kak-te-wahd-de	42
Figure 25.	Wooden Bowl	42
Figure 26.	Wooden Bowl	42
Figure 27.	Wooden Trencher	43
Figure 28.	Wooden Dish	43
Figure 29.	Wooden Bowl of Maple or Fir Knot	43
Figure 30.	Wooden Bowl of Maple or Fir Knot	43
Figure 31.	Conical Hat	45
Figure 32	Bark Basket	46
Figure 33.	Bow and Arrows	47
Figure 34.	Bird Spear	48
Figure 35.	Mask	69
Figure 36.	Mask	69
Figure 37.	Mask	69
Figure 38.	Mask	69
Figure 39.	Mask	70
Figure 40.	Mask	70
Figure 41.	Mask	70
Figure 42.	Dress of Female Performer in the *Tsiahk*	74
Figure 43.	Headdress of Male Performer in the *Tsiahk*	74
Figure 44.	Rattle used by Medicine Men	77

(ix)

THE INDIANS OF CAPE FLATTERY,

AT THE

ENTRANCE TO THE STRAIT OF FUCA, WASHINGTON TERRITORY.

THE tribe of Indians who inhabit the region about Cape Flattery is known among the whites and the Indians who reside further eastward, on the Straits of Fuca, as the Makah, or more properly speaking, Mak-kah, the word being strongly accented on both syllables. They are also called by the tribes on the western coast of Vancouver Island, "Klas-set," and by those tribes residing between the Columbia river and Cape Flattery, "Kwe-nět-sat'h." The tribal name among themselves is "Kwe-nět-che-chat." All these different names have the same meaning, and signify "the people who live on a point of land projecting into the sea," or, as we term it, the "Cape People." There are other tribes who reside on promontories, but the Makahs appear to be the only one who are particularly called "Cape Indians."

GEOGRAPHICAL POSITION.—At the time of making the treaty between the United States and the Makah Indians in 1855, known as the treaty of Neeah Bay, which was effected by Governor Isaac I. Stevens, of Washington Territory, who was also Superintendent of Indian Affairs, the tribe claimed as their land, all that portion of the extreme northwest part of Washington Territory lying between Flattery Rocks on the Pacific coast, fifteen miles south from Cape Flattery, and the Hoko river, about the same distance eastward from the cape on the Strait of Fuca. They also claimed Tatooche Island, which lies at the southern side of the entrance to the Strait, and separated from the main land of the cape by a channel half a mile wide.

This tract of country was ceded to the United States, except a portion of the extreme point of the cape, from Neeah Bay to the Wäatch creek on the Pacific, both points being nearly equally distant from Tatooche Island, say six miles each way. The reserved portion, as can be readily seen, by reference to the maps of the United States Coast Survey, is separated from the main body of the peninsula by a tract of swamp and meadow land, partially covered with a dense forest, and partially open marsh, extending from Neeah Bay to the Pacific, a distance of about four miles. The general appearance of this low land, and the abrupt and almost precipitous hills which border it on both sides through its entire length, show almost conclusively, that at a not very remote period, the waters of the Pacific joined those of Neeah Bay, leaving that portion of the cape which is included within the boundaries named by the treaty, an island. This hypothesis is supported by a tradition of the natives to that effect, which will be noticed in another portion of this paper. Even at the present time, the waters of Wäatch creek at very high tides, flow, by one of its branches, within a few rods of the waters of Neeah Bay. The whole of this region is of a mountainous character, and is the termination of the Olympic range, which has its highest peak far in the interior, near Hood's canal. From the snow-covered mountains in the rear of Dungeness, the range gradually becomes depressed, till at Cape Flattery it assumes the character of hills, five or six hundred feet in height. These hills are composed of conglomerate, clay-stone, tertiary sandstones, and occasional boulders of granite. Small veins of bituminous coal have been found on the cape, but as yet nothing of practical value. With but very few intervals, the whole of this portion of Washington Territory is covered with an almost impenetrable forest, which at Cape Flattery is composed of spruce and hemlock, and a dense undergrowth of crab apple, alder, elder, gualtheria, raspberry, wild currant, and rose bushes. The only land belonging to the Makahs, suitable for cultivation, is at Tsuess, where an open prairie of sandy loam affords material for farming; another open spot is on a hill at Flattery rocks, where the Indians cultivate some potatoes; and several acres at Neeah Bay have been cleared from the forest at great expense and labor, for the use of the Reservation officers and employés, who are stationed at that point. The Wäatch marsh is fit for a stock range only during the summer, and its best portions could not be cultivated save by extensively draining the land, and preparing it for the plough. The soil at Neeah Bay consists of a stiff clay loam and ridges of rich black earth, formed by the decomposition of the animal and vegetable matter thrown out by the Indians, and accumulated for centuries. The humidity of the climate is extreme, consequently the cereals do not ripen, nor has it been found possible to cure hay. Very excellent potatoes, however, are raised, and the soil and climate are well adapted to the growth, in perfection, of root vegetables of various kinds. The animals most common are elk, deer, black bears, wolves, beaver, otter, raccoons, skunks, minks, squirrels, etc. But these are found in limited numbers, although they abound in the interior. They are not much sought after by the Indians, who devote their attention more particularly to marine animals, such as fur and hair seal, porpoises, whales, and fish of various kinds, which are plentiful and form the principal part of their food.

CENSUS OF THE TRIBE.—During the month of October, 1861, I took a census of the Makah tribe, under the direction of the United States Indian Agent. This service was performed by visiting every lodge in the different villages, at a time when the whole tribe were in winter quarters. The villages at that time were Bäada and Neeah, at Neeah Bay; and Wäatch, Tsuess and Hosett, on the Pacific coast. There were six hundred and fifty-four souls, all told; viz., men, 205; women, 224; boys, 93; girls, 93; infants, 39. Again, in October, 1863, I took another census of the tribe for the Indian Department. The village of Bäada had then been removed within the limits of the Reserve, and joined with Neeah village. This census showed a table of 202 men, 232 women, 111 boys, 95 girls, and 23 infants, a total of six hundred and sixty-three. It appears from the above, that from 1861 to 1863, there had been but little change in the whole number, the births and deaths being nearly equal. While other tribes have been decreasing since 1852 (at which time the smallpox swept off a large number of them), this one seems to have been spared. The fact may be accounted for, in great measure, by their distance from the white settlements, and the small quantity of alcoholic poison which finds its way among them. But morally they are not at all in advance of their neighbors, and if the means of procuring whiskey were as readily at hand, they would soon become as degraded, and their numbers be as rapidly reduced, as the Chinook, Chihalis, Cowlitz, Clallam, Chemakum and other tribes of Washington Territory.

PHYSICAL CONSTITUTION.—The Makahs are of medium stature, averaging about five feet four inches; a few men of the tribe may be found who measure six feet, but only three or four of that height were noticed. Their limbs are commonly well proportioned, with a good development of muscle. Some are symmetrically formed, and of unusual strength. Although to a superficial observer they present much similarity of appearance, yet a further acquaintance, and closer examination, show that there is in reality a marked diversity. Some have black hair; very dark brown eyes, almost black; high cheek-bones, and dark copper-colored skin; others have reddish hair, and a few, particularly among the children, light flaxen locks, light brown eyes, and fair skin, many of them almost white—a fact perhaps attributable to an admixture of white blood of Spanish and Russian stock.[1]

The custom of flattening the forehead, as observed among the Chinook, Chihalis, and other tribes south of Cape Flattery, does not appear to be in general use among the Makahs. This practice is not common among the Clyoquot and Nootkans (Tokwaht) to the north, and as the Makahs have intermarried with the tribes both north and south, we find it confined principally to those families who are related to the Kwinaiults, Chihalis, and Clallams. It is not uncommon to see children, belonging to the same parents, some of whom have their heads as nature made them, while others are deformed by compressing them in infancy. I am not prepared to state positively what mental effect is produced by this compression of the skull, but from my own experience among the children there seems to be but little difference in their capacity for acquiring information, or in their desire for instruction; the most proficient, however, appear to be those with naturally formed heads. It would require an extended and close observation for a series of years, marking the growth of these children to mature age, and noting the various peculiarities of a number selected for the purpose, before any reliable results could be had on which to found a correct judgment.

---

[1] In Holmberg's Work will be found an account of the wreck of a Russian ship, the survivors of whose crew lived several years among the Makahs. As late as 1854, I saw their descendants, who bore in their features unmistakable evidence of their origin. (G. G.)

These Indians are not remarkable for the special perfection of any of their organs, as that of sight, or hearing, or smelling; or for any corporeal faculties, as speed in running, agility in climbing, or of diving and remaining long under water. I have seen them occasionally run foot-races on the beach, climb poles set up for the purpose, and swim and dive in the bay, but they do not excel in any of these athletic exercises. They do excel, however, in the management of canoes, and are more venturesome, hardy, and ardent in their pursuit of whales, and in going long distances from the land for fish, than any of the neighboring tribes. They are, in fact, to the Indian population what the inhabitants of Nantucket are to the people of the Atlantic coast, being the most expert and successful in the whale fishery of all the coast tribes.

They do not appear to be a very long-lived people. At the present time (1864) there is but one old man who was alive at the time the Spaniards attempted to make a settlement at Neeah Bay in 1792. He could remember the circumstance well a few years since, but is now in his dotage. He was then a small boy, and if we assume that he was but five years old, it would make him now seventy-seven years of age. I have inquired of a number of men whose appearance indicated advanced age, and with the exception above named, have found no one who personally recollected the visit of the Spaniards, although all remembered hearing their fathers mention it. Threescore years may be safely set down as the limit of life among those who escape the casualties incident to their savage condition; and, I think, from my observations among them, that an Indian at sixty years is as old as a white man at eighty. The average longevity is of course far below this standard, but I have no data that would warrant a positive statement of what that actually is; it could only be ascertained by an accurate record of births and deaths during a series of years.

DWELLINGS.—The houses of the Makahs are built of boards and planks, split from the cedar. These are principally made by the Indians of Vancouver Island, and procured by barter with them. There is very little cedar about Cape Flattery, and such as is found is small and of inferior quality. Drift logs, however, are frequently thrown on the shores by the high tides of winter, and whenever any such are saved they are either split into boards or made into canoes. The process of making the boards is very primitive. A number of long narrow wedges are cut from the yew, which is selected for its hardness; little rings of withes, made like a sail-maker's "grummet," are fastened on the head of the wedge to keep it from splitting under the blows of the stone hammer. These hammers are shaped like a pestle, and made from the hardest stone that can be found. They are very neatly formed, but the process is tedious and laborious. A description will be found under *Arts and Manufactures*. The Indian first strips the bark from the log, and cuts off the end as squarely as he can; he next cuts transversely through the top of the log, as far from the end as the required length of the plank, and as deep as the required thickness. A horizontal cut is then made across the end of the log with the axe, and into this are inserted the wedges, about three inches apart. These are struck successively with the stone hammer till the split is effected; more wedges are then inserted in the longitudinal split on each side of the board, and all being regularly driven in, the board comes off very straight. The first piece being rounded on the top, is a mere slab. The process is repeated until the log is entirely split up. The widest and best boards are from the centre, and are highly prized. I have measured some of them which were over five feet in width. The choicest are reserved for use in the interior of the lodge, or to paint their rude devices upon.

When a sufficient number of boards is procured, they next proceed to the erection of the house. The roofs of all these houses are nearly flat, the least possible inclination being given them that will allow the water to pass off freely. They are intended to accommodate several families, and are of various dimensions; some of them being sixty feet long by thirty wide, and from ten to fifteen feet high. To support the weight of these flat roofs it is necessary to have large timbers. These are usually hewn down evenly, and are set up, either parallel with the length of the house (in which case only one great timber extends along it), or else across the width, when three or four are used. A space of the required size having been cleared of stones and rubbish, and properly levelled, stout posts, notched on the top, are securely inserted perpendicularly into the ground. The friends and neighbors join to assist. Then all unite at one end of the beam and raise it as high as they can at one lift, when it is blocked up. Stout poles, with their ends lashed together crosswise, are now inserted under the beam, and while some hoist it, others are lifting at the poles, till finally, after excessive labor and waste of strength, the end of the timber is raised and placed on the top of the notched post; the other end of the beam is then raised, supporting posts are placed under the centre, and the first portion of the building is finished. Whenever one of these large beams is to be lifted, or when any work requiring the united exertions of several is to be done, it is usual for some one, generally an old man, to give the word. He may be seen at such times seated a little distance off, with a stick in his hand, with which to strike a blow on a board as a signal. When all is ready, he calls out "*Shaugh shogh*," which they all repeat, and at the word "*Shogh*" he gives a blow with his stick and all lift together. The expression is equivalent to "Now then, hoist!" or if to move a canoe, "Now then, haul!"

Other posts are next set in the ground, which serve to form the frame for the sides and ends. Smaller timbers are fixed on these posts parallel with the large one, then poles are placed at right angles across the whole, and on these are lastly laid the roof boards, which are made slightly concave on one side and convex on the other, and are set alternately, overlapping like tiles. The sides and ends are now to be built up with boards. First, double rows of poles are set up perpendicularly all around the house, at distances of four or five feet from each other, the rows themselves being about four inches apart. A board is then placed between these rows of poles, with one of its edges resting on the ground. Withes made from twisted cedar twigs are passed round the poles, and on these withes another board is laid, with its lower edge overlapping the one beneath; this process is repeated till the sides and ends are complete. Moss and dry sea-weed are then stuffed into all the seams, and the house is considered habitable.

The bed places are next to the walls of the house, and raised about eighteen inches from the ground; on them are laid Clallam mats, which, being made of bulrushes and flags, are better adapted for sleeping upon than the cedar bark mats of their own manufacture. These mats are rolled up at one end of the bed so as to form a pillow, and on them the Indian lies down, with generally no other covering than the blanket he has worn through the day. Sometimes a thickness of eight or ten mats is used, but commonly from three to five. They make a very healthy and easy couch by themselves, but some of the more luxurious add a sack full of feathers. These bed places are arranged all around the sides and ends of the lodges, and are separated from each other by the boxes containing the family wealth, consisting of blankets, beads, and clothing, which are piled up at the head and feet. Directly in front of them is a lower platform, usually three inches from the ground. On this, other mats are laid, and here the family and visitors sit and eat or talk as the case may be. The fire is in front of it, and a chain depending from a beam overhead, serves to hang the pots or kettles on, while cooking. Over the beds are stowed the provisions belonging to the family, packed away in baskets, while above the fire are hung such fish or other food as they may be desirous of drying in the smoke.

The dwellings of the Makahs are not removed except for some emergency. They are collected in villages, each containing from eight to fifteen houses. The principal one is situated at Neeah, to which locality that formerly at Bäada, on the eastern point of the bay, has been removed, and the two thus combined comprise fifteen dwellings and two hundred and forty-one inhabitants. The other villages are Wäatch, on the Pacific coast, at the mouth of Wäatch creek, four miles from Neeah, consisting of nine dwellings and one hundred and twenty-six residents; Tsuess, four miles south from Wäatch, containing eight houses and ninety-nine residents, and Hosett, at Flattery Rocks, consisting of fifteen houses and one hundred and eighty-eight persons. The above constitute the winter residences of the tribe. Early in the spring they remove to their summer quarters, which are the villages of Kiddekubbut, three miles from Neeah; Tatooche Island, and Ahchawat, between Tatooche Island and Wäatch. At these three spots are houses, similar to those in the other villages, which are left standing when the tribe goes into winter quarters. Occasionally, when an Indian has not sufficient boards for both, he will remove the roof-boards to whichever house he is occupying. To do so, they place two canoes abreast and lay the boards across the top. Each house is generally owned by one individual, and the families who occupy it with him are his relatives or friends, who are accommodated free of rent. They usually, however, make presents of food, or render assistance in various ways when required; but they are not obliged to do either unless they wish. The houses are all placed fronting the beach, and usually have but one door. Some, however, have a small opening in the rear, through which wood and water are brought in. They have no buildings set apart for public purposes, but when an unusually large gathering takes place, they proceed to the largest lodge, which is always thrown open for the accommodation of the tribe.

The reason why the roofs of the houses are so different from those of the Chihalis and Chinooks, at the Columbia river, is that they are used to dry fish upon. Now, the Chinooks and Chihalis, as well as all the tribes on the sound and

THE INDIANS OF CAPE FLATTERY.

coast, store great quantities of fish for their winter's use; but the fish they dry are salmon, which require to be cured in the smoke and protected from the sun and rain. Consequently, the tribes above mentioned use pitched roofs, or roofs much more elevated than those of the Makahs. But the staple of the Makahs is halibut, which, to be properly cured, is cut into thin slices and dried, if possible, in the open air without smoke; the best portions being those that have kept white and free from any color. As the climate is very humid, it is rare that a season is propitious for the curing their fish; so they have their roofs as flat as possible, and during fair weather, in the fishing season, not only are these covered with the slices of fish, but quantities are hung on horizontal poles fastened across the ends of the uprights that form the side fastenings to the houses. The appearance of one of the lodges on a fine day in summer when plenty of fish are drying is that of a laundry with clothes out bleaching. When the weather threatens to be rainy, the occupants proceed to the roof, and by removing several boards, they can stow away their provender in a very few minutes, and again replace it in the open air on the return of fair weather.

The interior of a lodge often presents a curious domestic scene. In one corner may be seen a mother rocking her child to sleep, securely lashed in its cradle, which is suspended by strings to the top of a pliant pole, that moves with every motion of her hand. If the mother is engaged in making baskets or mats, she transfers the string from her hand to her great toe, and moving her foot, produces the required motion, not unlike that of a modern baby jumper. In the centre a chain hangs from the roof, supporting over the fire the kettle in which is the food for her husband, while a boy, having cooked his own meal, is taking it alone. In another part of the house, separated from this apartment by a board set up on edge to serve as a partition, is another family, the father holding an infant in his arms, while another child is playing with kittens; the child's mother seated on the bed, wrapped in her blanket, and a group of friends in the centre cooking their supper.

PICTURE WRITING.—In almost every lodge may be seen large boards or planks of cedar carefully smoothed and painted with rude designs of various kinds. With one exception, however, I have found nothing of a legendary or historic character, their drawings being mostly representations of the private totem or tamanous of individuals, and consisting of devices rarely understood by their owners and never by any one else. The exception referred to is a representation of the thunder-bird (T'hlu-klŭts), the whale (chet-up-ŭk), and the fabulous animal supposed by the natives to cause lightning (Ha-hék-to-ak). This painting is on a large board in the lodge of one of the chiefs of Neeah Bay, and was executed by a Clyoquot Indian named "Chá-tik," a word signifying painter or artist. A painting is termed Cha-tái-ūks, and writing Chá-tātl.

The coast Indians, as well as those I have conversed with, living on Puget Sound, believe that thunder is caused by an immense bird whose size darkens the heavens, and the rushing of whose wings produces peals of thunder. The Makahs, however, have a superstition which invests the thunder-bird with a twofold character. This mythological being is supposed by them to be a gigantic Indian, named, in the various dialects of the coast tribes, Ka-kaitch, T'hlu-klūts, and Tu-tūtsh, the latter being the Nootkan name. This giant lives on the highest mountains, and his food consists of whales. When he is in want of food, he puts on a garment consisting of a bird's head, a pair of immense wings, and a feather covering for his body; around his waist he ties the Ha-hĕk-to-ak, or lightning fish, which bears some faint resemblance to the sea horse (*hippocampus*). This animal has a head as sharp as a knife, and a red tongue which makes the fire. The T'hlu-klūts having arrayed himself, spreads his wings and sails over the ocean till he sees a whale. This he kills by darting the Ha-hĕk-to-ak down into its body, which he then seizes in his powerful claws and carries away into the mountains to eat at his leisure. Sometimes the Ha-hĕk-to-ak strikes a tree with his sharp head, splitting and tearing it in pieces, or again, but very rarely, strikes a man and kills him. Whenever lightning strikes the land or a tree, the Indians hunt very diligently with the hope of finding some portion of the Ha-hĕk-to-ak, for the possession of any part of this marvellous animal endows its owner with great powers, and even a piece of its bone, which is supposed by the Indians to be bright red, will make a man expert in killing whales, or excel in any kind of work. Those Indians, however, who pretend to possess these fabulous relics carefully conceal them from sight, for they are considered as great "medicines," and not to be seen except by the possessor. A tale was related to me, and religiously believed by them, respecting the possession of a quill of the thunder bird by a Kwinaiult Indian, now living, named Neshwāts. He was hunting on a mountain near Kwinaiult, and saw a thunder bird light on a rock. Creeping up softly, he succeeded in securing a buckskin thong to one of its wing feathers, fastening the other end at the same time to a stump. When the T'hlu-klūts flew off, the feather was drawn from the wing and kept by the Indian. The length of this enormous feather is forty fathoms. Neshwāts is very careful that no person shall see this rare specimen, but his tale is believed, particularly as he is very expert in killing sea otter, which abound on that part of the coast.

I saw an instance of their credulity on an occasion of a display of fireworks at Port Townsend a few summers since. A number of the rockets on bursting displayed fiery serpents. The Indians believed they were Ha-hĕk-to-ak, and for a long time made application to the gentlemen who gave the display, for pieces of the animal, for which they offered fabulous prices. So firm is their belief in this imaginary animal, that one chief assured me if I could procure him a backbone he would give two hundred dollars for it. One of the principal residences of the T'hlu-klūts is on a mountain back of Clyoquot, on Vancouver Island. There is a lake situated in the vicinity, and around its borders the Indians say are quantities of old bones of whales. These, they think, were carried there by the T'hlu-klūts, but they are very old, and it must have been many years ago. I have not seen these bones, but have heard of them from various Indians who allege that they have seen them. If they really do exist as stated, they are undoubtedly the fossil remains that have been deposited there at a time when that portion of the continent was submerged, and respecting which there is a tradition still among them. The painting above described, although done by an Indian, does not fully represent the idea of the Makahs respecting the T'hlu-klūts. But, having by me a copy of Kitto's Cyclopædia of Biblical Literature, I showed some of the chiefs the cut of the Babylonian cherubim, which came very near their idea of its real form. It was perfect, they said, with the exception of not having the Ha-hék-to-ak around its waist, and of having feet instead of bird's claws, which they think are necessary to grasp whales. But when I informed them that there were no whales in Babylon, they were fully persuaded that the identity was the same, claws being given to the T'hlu-klūts who live near water, and feet to those living in the interior. Of their religious belief in this thunder-bird, I shall make further mention in their ta-ma-na-was ceremonies. In the design the T'hlu-klūts is represented as holding a whale in its talons, and the accompanying figures are the Ha-hék-to-ak. These animals the bird is supposed to collect from the ocean, and keep concealed in its feathers.

Fig. 1.

Thunder-bird of the Makahs.

Among the most remarkable specimens of their painting which I have seen, was a design on the conical hats worn during rain, and another on a board in a chief's lodge, afterwards placed at the base of a monument erected over his body. The circular design for the hat was said to represent a pair of eyes, a nose, and mouth. The other was a rude one, in which eyes are very conspicuous. The form of these designs is a distinctive feature in Indian painting, but I never could learn that they attached any more meaning to them than we do to the designs on a shawl border, or the combinations of a calico pattern artist.[1]

I have painted various devices for these Indians, and have decorated their ta-ma-na-was masks; and in every instance I was simply required to paint something the Indians had never seen before. One Indian selected from a pictorial newspaper a cut of a Chinese dragon, and another chose a double-headed eagle, from a picture of an Austrian coat-of-arms. Both these I grouped with drawings of crabs, faces of men, and various devices, endeavoring to make the whole look like Indian work; and I was very successful in giving the most entire satisfaction, so much so that they bestowed upon me the name of Chā-tic, intimating that I was as great an

---

[1] The constant recurrence of certain conventional figures in the ornamentation of all the tribes from Cape Flattery to Sitka would seem to indicate a symbolical meaning, now lost. Examples may be found in the Clyoquot paddle; in the trencher and dish; and two of the masks, *post*. (G. G.)

artist as the Chä-tic of Clyoquot. In the masks I painted, I simply endeavored to form as hideous a mixture of colors as I could conceive, and in this I again gave satisfaction.

I have noticed in Indian paintings executed by the northern tribes, particularly the Chimsyan, Haida, and others north of Vancouver Island, a very great resemblance in style to that adopted by the coast Indians. Whether or not these tribes have any legend connected with their pictures I have no means of ascertaining. There are, however, but very few persons among the coast Indians who are recognized as painters, and those that I have met with, either could not or would not give me any explanation. My object in painting for them was to find out if they really had any historical or mythological ideas which they wished to have represented, and I have invariably inquired on every occasion; but I never could get any other information than that they wished me to paint something the other Indians could not understand. I am satisfied, so far as this tribe is concerned, that, with the exception of the thunder-bird drawing, all their pictures and drawings are nothing more than fancy work, or an attempt to copy some of the designs of the more northern tribes; and as they have always evinced a readiness to explain to me whatever had significance, I have no alternative but to believe them when they say that they attach no particular meaning to their paintings.

SOCIAL LIFE.—The Makahs, in common with all the coast tribes, hold slaves. These were formerly procured by making captives of the children or adults of any other tribes with whom they might be at variance. But latterly, since the advent of the whites, they have obtained their slaves mostly by purchase from their neighbors on Vancouver Island, or those further up the Strait of Fuca. Children seem in all cases to be preferred, because they are cheaper, and are less likely to escape than adults. The price varies, according to age, from fifty to one hundred blankets. These slaves are for the most part well treated, and, but for the fact that they can be bought and sold, appear to be on terms of equality with their owners, although there are instances where they have received rather harsh usage. In case one is killed by his master, which occasionally happens, no notice is taken of the occurrence by the rest of the tribe. Many of the men who were born of slave parents, and have resided all their lives with the tribe, have purchased their freedom; while others, who were bought, when children, from other tribes, have regained their liberty as soon as they have grown up, by making their escape. In fact the only slaves who are sure to remain are those who are born in the tribe; all others will run away whenever a safe opportunity presents to enable them to get back to their relatives. In former times, it is said, the slaves were treated very harshly, and their lives were of no more value than those of dogs. On the death of a chief, his favorite slaves were killed and buried with him, but latterly, this custom seems to have been abandoned, and their present condition is a mild kind of servitude. The treaty between the United States and the Makahs makes it obligatory on this tribe to free their slaves, and although this provision has not thus far been enforced, it has had the effect of securing to the latter better treatment than they formerly had. Instances are not rare where a master has married his slave woman, and a mistress has taken her slave man as her husband. The children

THE INDIANS OF CAPE FLATTERY.

of such connections are considered half slave, and although some of the more intelligent have acquired wealth and influence among the tribe, yet the fact that the father or mother was a slave is considered as a stigma, which is not removed for several generations. Their status, as compared with the African slavery of the Southern States, is rather that of bond servants; they are the hewers of wood and drawers of water. They appear to have no task-work assigned them, but pursue the same avocations as their owners; the men assisting in the fisheries, and the women in manufacturing mats and baskets, and other indoor work, or in preparing and curing fish. Formerly, it was considered degrading for a chief, or the owner of slaves, to perform any labor except hunting, fishing, or killing whales; proficiency in any of these exercises was a consideration that enabled the most expert to aspire to the honor of being a chief or head man; but since the tribe has been under the charge of an agent of the Government, and it is seen that no distinction is made between bond or free, but that both are treated alike, the old prejudice against labor is wearing away, and men and women, with the exception of a few among the old chiefs, are willing to engage side by side in such work as requires to be done for the agency. And it is to be hoped that, in a few years, under the judicious plan of the treaty, slavery will be gradually abolished, or exist only in a still milder form. The division of labor between husband and wife, or between the males and females, is, that the men do all the hunting and fishing, and cut the firewood. The women dress and cure the fish or game, bring wood and water, and carry all burdens of whatever nature that require transportation. They also attend to the household duties of preparing and cooking food; but the men wash and mend their own clothes, and in many instances make them. This custom is not confined to the slaves, but is practised by all. The women also provide a portion of the food, such as berries and various edible roots, and, to a limited extent, cultivate potatoes. The fact that they assist in procuring food, appears to secure for them better treatment by the men, than is usual among the buffalo-hunting tribes east of the Rocky Mountains. The husband, however, claims the privilege of correcting the wife, and some of them receive very severe beatings; but, on the other hand, they have the privilege of leaving their husbands, which they do for a slight cause. The marriage tie is but a slender bond, which is easily sundered, although it requires much negotiation when first contracted. Among the common people it is simply a purchase, payment being made in blankets, canoes, and guns, or such other commodities as may be agreed upon; but where the girl is the daughter or relative of a chief, a variety of ceremonies takes place. One of these, which I have witnessed, displayed a canoe borne on the shoulders of eight men, and containing three persons, one in the bow of the craft in the act of throwing a whaling harpoon at the door of a lodge; one in the centre about to cast a seal-skin buoy, which was attached to the harpoon; and one in the stern with a paddle as if steering. The ceremonies in this instance represented the manner of taking a whale.

The procession formed on the beach a short distance from the lodge, and in front of it an Indian, dressed in a blanket which concealed his head, crept on all fours, occasionally raising his body to imitate a whale when blowing. At intervals the Indian in the canoe would throw the harpoon as if to strike, taking studious care, however, not to hit him; then the same evolutions were performed as is customary in the whale fishery. A party of friends followed the canoe, who sang to the accompaniment of drums and rattles. The burthen of their song was, that they had come to purchase a wife for one of their number, and recounted his merits and the number of blankets he would pay. When they reached the lodge the representative of the whale moved to one side, while the man in the canoe threw his harpoon with such force as to split the door, which was a single plank, in halves. The door, however, was kept barred, and the party, after piling a great number of blankets and a couple of guns against it, rested awhile, hoping to be admitted. After another chant, and the adding of a few more blankets to the heap, another harpoon was thrown against the door; but to no purpose, the damsel was obdurate, and the price not sufficient to satisfy her parents. This operation may be said to be symbolical of Cupid's dart on a large scale. The party effected nothing, and returned home. A few weeks later another lover, who was acceptable to the girl, came from Nittinat on Vancouver Island, with a great number of friends in five large canoes. These approached the shore, side by side, very slowly, the Indians in them standing up, singing and brandishing their paddles; they stopped just outside the surf, and one of the men delivered a speech, stating what they had come for and what they would pay. Then they all landed, and, having hauled their canoes on the beach, formed a blanket procession. First came a ta-má-na-was or medicine man, dressed up with a gaudy display of finery, with his face painted red, and a bunch of eagle's feathers in his hair, a large wooden rattle in one hand and a bunch of scallop shells in the other, with which he kept time to a song. Next him was a man with a blanket over one shoulder, and holding one corner of another blanket, which was stretched out by an Indian who walked behind him holding the other corner, and also the corner of a third blanket, which was in like manner held by a third Indian behind. In this manner eighty-four blankets were brought by the procession, single file, and deposited one after the other at the door of the lodge, which in this instance was open, showing that the suitor was favorably received; but the eighty-four blankets were not enough, so the procession returned to the canoes and brought eighty-four more blankets in the same manner. These were all piled up outside the lodge; but the parents were in no haste, their daughter was too valuable, and the lover must wait. This he did for a week with all his friends. Every day a speech was made, and every night songs and dances were performed. At length the parents yielded, and the maiden was carried off in triumph, very much to her own satisfaction as well as that of her lover. The blankets, guns, and other articles used in the purchase, are not usually retained by the parents or relatives of the bride, but are returned to the bridegroom, who takes them home with his new wife and distributes them to the friends of both. In short, what is said to be paid for a wife, is simply the amount which the bridegroom will give away to the assembled friends.

A girl is considered marriageable as soon as she arrives at puberty. On the appearance of the menstrual discharge she is immediately secluded, by being placed behind a screen of mats or boards in a corner of the lodge. A number of little girls are in attendance day and night for a week or ten days, who keep up a constant singing. They relieve each other as they get tired; but the girl is never left alone, nor do the songs cease except at slight intervals. At the expiration of this first period, the girl is taken out to be washed. The little girls form a procession, at the head of which she walks, with her face concealed in her blanket, the children singing as loud as they can scream. Arrived at the brook she is required to sit naked in the cold water half an hour, and is then taken back to the lodge. She is bathed in this manner three times a day for a fortnight, and her hair tied up in two bunches, one on each side of her head, which are wound round with cloth, strips of leather, beads, brass buttons, and other trinkets. The only dress worn is a cincture of fringed bark about the waist, reaching to the knee, and a blanket. At the expiration of a month the ordinary dress is resumed, and a headdress of the shells of the dentalium put on. This is the distinctive mark of all young girls until they are married. After this first period they are not compelled to live apart on the monthly return, nor are they required to be secluded after giving birth to a child. Love matches are frequently made, and whenever the parents are opposed the young couple will hide themselves in the woods for a day or two, and on their return the matter is amicably arranged.

Marriages usually take place at an early period. The men take for wives either the women of their own or the neighboring tribes; but they are prohibited from marrying any of their own connections, unless the consanguinity is very remote. I do not know of an instance nearer than a fourth cousin. I knew of one young man who was in love with his own cousin, and the Indians spoke of it to me in terms of contempt; they said he wanted to marry his sister, and it was not permitted. Polygamy is practised among the Makahs, but is not general. None of them, however, have more than two wives, and these are on terms of perfect equality. If one thinks herself ill treated, she will leave and get another husband, in which event she will take her children with her. If the wife dies, the father takes the children; but while the mother lives and they need her care, she invariably takes them with her to her new abode. The facility with which the wives can leave their husbands and take others, gives rise to great confusion, particularly to the mind of a stranger seeking information relative to their domestic affairs. Chastity among the females is a thing much talked of, but it appears to be more honored in the breach than the observance, and, although they are not so grossly licentious as the Clallams and other tribes on the Sound, yet the men have great occasion for jealousy.

The festivals are but few, and are confined to the ta-má-na-was ceremonies, which usually take place during the winter months; to certain "medicine" performances, which will be alluded to hereafter, both of these closing with feasting and dancing, and the pot-lat-ches, or distributions of presents, which are made at all seasons of the year. The-ta-má-na-was is allied to a religious ceremony, and will be treated of under that head. The pot-lat-ches occur whenever an Indian has acquired enough property in blankets, beads, guns, brass kettles, tin pans, and other objects of Indian wealth, to make a present to a large number of the tribe; for the more an Indian can give away, the greater his standing with the others, and the better his chance of attaining to the dignity of a chief among his people.

Whenever it is the intention of an individual to make such a distribution of his property, a number of his friends are called in solemn council; an inventory of the articles is made, and the amount each one is to receive is decided upon. The names of the persons who are to be thus favored are then announced in the following manner: One of the party, seated on the ground with a board before him and a stick in his hand, acts as a herald. The person about to give the presents then announces a name, which, if satisfactory to the assembled friends, is repeated, whereupon the herald strikes a blow on the board with his stick, and calls the name in a loud voice; this is repeated until all the names are called to whom presents are to be given, and the articles each is to receive decided upon. Messengers are then sent to invite the guests. If the party is to be a large one, there will be from fifteen to twenty messengers who go in a body, with painted faces, and sprigs of evergreen in their hair. They enter the lodges with songs, and one of their number announces the intended feast and calls aloud the names of all who are invited. On the set day these assemble at the lodge of the Indian who gives the entertainment, and, after much feasting, singing, dancing, and masquerade performance, which sometimes lasts several days, the articles are distributed. The blankets are displayed on poles, or cords stretched across the lodge for the purpose, and all the other articles are placed so as to be seen by the assembled guests, who are seated at one end of the lodge opposite the goods. The herald, after making a speech, extolling the great liberality of the donor, strikes the board with his stick, and calls a name; thereupon an attendant takes the intended present and deposits it in front of the person who is to receive it, where it remains till all are served. Then a song is sung, a dance performed, and the party retire.

Sometimes these parties are composed of children. The parents of a boy or girl who are ambitious for the child, give presents to the children of the tribe. Invitations are sent to the parents, and the names of those children who are to receive the offerings are given. The entertainments are similar to those in the case of adults, except that the performers are children, who dance and sing and go through a variety of plays. The dancing is certainly not graceful; it consists in a clumsy sort of jump, with about as much ease and agility as a person would display while attempting to dance in a sack. The children have a variety of plays, some of which resemble those of white children, and were undoubtedly learned by observation of the customs of those they have seen at Victoria and other places on the Strait and Sound. For instance, peg-tops, which they call ba-bet'hl-ká-di, and battledore and shuttlecock, which is termed kla-há-tla (kla-hăk, shuttlecock; kó-ko-wi, battledore). They also make little wagons, using for wheels sections of kelp stems, cut transversely and about an inch thick. These stems are cylindrical and hollow, and the little wheels answer exceedingly well for their miniature carts. They are quite as expert as most white children in the manufacture of miniature ships and schooners; some of which are very creditable pieces of work. But their chief pleasure is to get into a little canoe, just large enough to float them, and paddle about in the surf. It is this early and constant practice in the management of a canoe and the use of the paddle, that makes them so exceedingly expert when they become of maturer years. Another pastime of the boys is to imitate the killing of a whale. One will select a kelp stem of the largest size, and trail it along the beach. The other boys, armed with miniature harpoons with wooden buoys attached, follow after, and dart their harpoons into the kelp, until it is full or split, when they get another, and keep up the game with eagerness for hours. Another sport is to set a pole upright in the sand and climb to the top, which they do readily by tying a piece of rope so as to form a loop, which is passed once around the pole, forming stirrups for the feet. As they climb, the rope is slipped up by the feet, but becomes fast on pressing the weight upon it; this affords a foothold, till the hands are raised for a fresh grasp of the pole, when the feet are again lifted, and thus alternately by hands and feet, they rapidly ascend to the top. The use of the bow and arrow is early learned by the boys, and is a favorite source of amusement. A description of them will be found under *Arts and Manufactures*. The amusements of the girls consist in dressing up clam shells with strips of rags, and setting them in rows in the sand to resemble children. They are also very fond of dolls, and appear much pleased with any toys such as white children use. They are early taught to make little baskets and mats, and their simple sports are varied by excursions into the woods after berries, or among the rocks, at low tide, in search of shell fish. Like the boys, they are accustomed from infancy to the use of canoes, and may be seen on any pleasant day throughout the summer, paddling in any pool of water left by the receding tide, or in the little bays formed at the mouths of the brooks by the sand which may have been washed in during high water. During the spring, when the flowers are in bloom and the humming birds are plenty, the boys take a stick smeared with the slime from snails, and place it among a cluster of flowers. This slime is an excellent bird lime, and if a humming bird applies his tongue to it he is glued fast. They will then tie a piece of thread to its feet and holding the other end let the birds fly, their humming being considered quite an amusement. They however are cruel to all animals, and particularly birds, which they torture in every conceivable manner. Among their sports is wrestling, which is common not only with the boys but the men also. The parties are entirely naked, and at a signal advance and seize each other by the hair. Each then strives to throw his antagonist, and the victor is rewarded by the shouts of his friends.

Formerly, deadly combats or duels were often fought. Each fighter being armed with a dagger held in the right hand, grasps firmly with the left the long hair of his antagonist; then holding each other fast, they inflict wounds with their knives till one or both are mortally wounded, or else both are exhausted, when friends interfere and the parties are separated. Some fighting is done with big stones instead of knives, when each tries to beat the other's brains out; but these gladiatorial scenes are of very rare occurrence of late years. The most common practice in vogue at present is shooting each other with guns or pistols.

DRESS.—The usual dress of the men consists of a shirt and blanket; but some, especially the old men, are content with a blanket only. Nearly all of them however have suits of clothes of various kinds, which they have procured from the whites; but these are only worn on occasions of visits to the settlements up the Strait, on the arrival of strangers, or when at work for the white people, and are usually taken off when they return to their lodges. It is not an unusual sight to see an Indian who has been well dressed, even to stockings and shoes or boots, perhaps for several days while with white people, or who may have been at work all day, come out of his lodge at night, or as soon as he leaves work, with nothing on but a blanket. This change from warm clothing to nearly none at all causes colds and coughs to be prevalent among them. During rainy weather they wear, in addition to the blanket, a conical hat woven from spruce roots, so compact as to exclude water, and a bear skin thrown over the shoulders. They are not particular in the arrangement of their dress, even when they have clothes to put on, and may occasionally be seen parading with a cap on the head, boots on the feet, and the body only covered with a blanket.

Fig. 2.

Makah Indian with his wet-weather fishing dress, blanket, bear skin, and hat.

Fig. 3.

Head dress and pendant of dentalium.

Before blankets of wool were procured from the whites, their dress was composed of robes made of skins or blankets woven from dogs' hair or from the prepared bark of the pine which is found on Vancouver Island. Very comfortable blankets were also made from the down of birds woven on strings to form the warp. These garments are still occasionally worn, and a description of their manufacture may be found under the proper head.

The dress of the women usually consists of a shirt or long chemise reaching from the neck to the feet; some have in addition, a skirt of calico like a petticoat tied around the waist, or petticoats made of blankets or coarse baize. Formerly their entire dress was merely a blanket and a cincture of fringed bark, reaching from the waist to the knees. This is called wad-dish, a name they apply to their petticoats of all kinds. Some of the women, particularly the younger ones, have of late years dressed themselves in calico gowns, which are always of an antique pattern and open in front instead of the back. Occasionally a squaw who has been to Victoria and seen the fashions of white women will array herself in hoops, but these articles, so necessary to the dress of civilized females, together with bonnets, are not at all becoming to a squaw, and it is doubtful whether the fashion will ever obtain among these natives. A Makah belle is considered in full dress with a clean chemise; a calico or woollen skirt; a plaid shawl of bright colors thrown over her shoulders; six or seven pounds of glass beads of various colors and sizes on strings about her neck; several yards of beads wound around her ankles; a dozen or more bracelets of brass wire around each wrist; a piece of shell pendent from her nose; ear ornaments composed of the shells of the dentalium, beads and strips of leather, forming a plait three or four inches wide and two feet long; and her face and the parting of the hair painted with grease and vermilion. The effect of this combination of colors and materials is quite picturesque, which is perhaps the only praise that it merits.

Both sexes have their noses pierced, and usually, although not constantly, suspended from them a small piece of the *haliotis* shell (the "abalone" of the Californians), obtained from Vancouver Island, particularly on the eastern side in the Cowitchin district, where specimens of a large size are found. Some wear pieces of this shell two or three inches square as ear ornaments. The men wear their hair long, but on whaling excursions they tie it up in a club knot behind the head. They frequently decorate themselves by winding wreaths of evergreens around the knob, or stick in a sprig of spruce with a feather. At times they vary this head-dress by substituting a wreath of sea-weed, or a bunch of cedar bark bound around the head like a turban. They paint their faces either black or red, as fancy may suggest, or in stripes of various colors. I have never been able to discover any particular signification for this practice, although I have frequently inquired. Some have told me the red paint was to keep the sun from burning their faces; others paint themselves black, either to show that they have stout and courageous hearts, or because they feel depressed; and others again because they happen to be in the humor of so doing. The method of painting is first to rub the face well with deer's tallow, upon which they apply the dry vermilion or red ochre if these colors are desired. If they wish to produce black, pulverized charcoal is first mixed with bear's grease or deer's fat, and rubbed between the hands, and then applied to the face. The other colors are put on dry. The mode of coloring the face in stripes is to dip a thin slip of wood in the dry paint and lay it carefully on the face, producing a red mark the width of the stick; narrow marks or lines are made with the edge of the stick. The lines thus drawn are more uniform and more clearly defined than if laid on with a brush, and are done quite rapidly. During the berry season the children paint or stain their faces with the juice. A coarse quality of red ochre is often used for painting their faces, and also the inside of canoes. This pigment is made by the Kwilléyute Indians, who reside thirty miles south from Cape Flattery. It is found in the form of a yellowish clay or ochre, which oozes in a semifluid state from the banks of the river at certain places. This is collected, squeezed into balls the size of a hen's egg, and then wrapped in rags and baked in the hot ashes till it acquires the desired hue. If heated too much the color becomes a dark brown, and is not so highly prized. When used it is pulverized and mixed with oil, for painting canoes, or applied dry to the face like vermilion, although some blend it first with grease and rub it between the palms of the hands before applying it. Another paint is made from hemlock bark found on decayed roots, or in the forks of old roots that have been long under ground. This is dried at the fire, and, to be used, is rubbed on a stone with spittle and then applied to the face. They all prefer vermilion, however, when they can get it, nor are they averse to using blue or yellow when they can procure those colors dry, which they occasionally do from the whites. During the grand ta-má-na-was or duk-wal-ly performances the face is painted black, and a wreath of cedar bark dyed red is worn around the head. During the tsi-āk or medicine ta-má-na-was the face is painted red, and the wreath is of undyed bark. This bark, which is prepared by beating it fine, is termed he-sé-yu. The name of the bark which has been dried but not broken is pīt-sōp. The war paint is generally black, although some use red; but the braves use black invariably. The hair is twisted in a knot behind, and green twigs tied up with it. The tattooing consists of marks on the arms or legs, and does not seem to amount to much. It is done by drawing a threaded needle under the skin, the thread having previously been colored with charcoal and water. Some prick in the color with a number of needles tied together, as sailors tattoo themselves. Many of these marks are merely straight lines, others show a rude attempt to represent an animal, and letters of the alphabet are sometimes seen tattooed on the arms, the characters being copied from any old newspaper they may get hold of. They seem to attach no definite meaning to this tattooing, and most of it is done while they are children. Many have no marks at all on their persons, while others have a few on the wrists and hands, and some on the ankles; but there is nothing in their tattooing which is in any way distinctive of tribe.

Some of the tribes on the northwest part of Vancouver Island have the custom of wearing disks of wood or ivory in the under lip, and I have seen it asserted that it is the custom of all the tribes from the Columbia River north. This however is not the fact with any of the coast tribes as far as I have seen, which is from the Columbia River to Nootka. The practice of flattening the heads of infants, although, as I have said, not universal among the Makahs, is performed in a manner similar to that of the Chinooks and other tribes in the vicinity of the Columbia River. As soon as a child is born it is washed with warm urine, and then smeared with whale oil and placed in a cradle made of bark, woven basket fashion; or of wood, either cedar or alder, hollowed out for the purpose. Into the cradle a quantity of finely separated cedar bark of the softest texture is first thrown. At the foot is a board raised at an angle of about 25°, which serves to keep the child's feet elevated; or, when the cradle is raised to allow the child to nurse, to form a support for the body, or a sort of seat. This is also covered with bark, he-sé-yu. A pillow is formed of the same material, just high enough to keep the head in its natural position, with the spinal column neither elevated nor depressed. First the child is laid on its back, its legs properly extended, its arms put close to its sides, and a covering either of bark or cloth laid over it; and then, commencing at the feet, the whole body is firmly laced up so that it has no chance to move in the least. When the body is well secured a padding of he-sé-yu is placed on the child's forehead, over which is laid bark of a somewhat stiffer texture, and the head is firmly lashed down to the sides of the cradle; thus the infant remains, seldom taken out more than once a day while it is very young, and then only to wash it and dry its bedding. The male children have a small opening left in the covering, through which the penis protrudes to enable them to void their urine. The same style of cradle appears to be used whether it is intended to compress the skull or not, and that deformity is accomplished by simply drawing the strings of the head-pad tightly and keeping up the pressure for a long time. Children are usually kept in these cradles till they are a year old, but as their growth advances they are not tied up quite so long as for the first few months. The mother, in washing her child, seldom takes the trouble to heat water; she simply fills her mouth with the water, and when she thinks it warm enough spirts it on the child and rubs it with her hand. If the child is very dirty, and they generally get thoroughly grimed up with soot and grease, a wash of stale urine is used, which effectually removes the oil and dirt, but does not impart a fragrant odor. This species of alkali as a substitute for soap is the general accompaniment of the morning toilet of both males and females. They wash as soon as they get up, and may be seen any morning proceeding to the brook with their urinals in their hands. In the winter months, in stormy weather, when they have been confined to the house, or after they have been curing fish or trying out oil, they get exceedingly dirty, and then they go through a process of scouring themselves with a wisp of grass or cedar leaves and sand and urine; after which they give themselves a rinse in fresh water and come out as red as boiled lobsters. Although, in respect of bathing, they may be said to be comparatively cleanly, yet they are not so particular about washing their clothes, which they wear till they are positively filthy before they will take the trouble to cleanse them; and as their washing is done in cold water, with but little if any soap, their clothes have always a dingy appearance. There are exceptions, however, to this, both among the males and females, particularly the younger ones, who, since the advent of the whites, seem more desirous of having clean apparel than their elders, who retain all their old savage customs.

FOOD, AND METHOD OF PROCURING IT.—The principal subsistence of the Makahs is drawn from the ocean, and is formed of nearly all its products, the most important of which are the whale and halibut. Of the former there are several varieties which are taken at different seasons of the year. Some are killed by the Indians; others, including the right whale, drift ashore, having been killed either by whalemen, sword fish, or other casualties. The various species of whales are: The sperm whale, kōts-ké, which is very rarely seen; right whale, yakh'-yo-bad-di; black fish, klas-ko-kop-ph; fin-back, kaú-wid; sulphur bottom, kwa-kwau-yak'-t'hle; California gray, che-che-wid, or chet'-a-pūk; killer, se-hwau. The generic name of whales is chet'-a-pūk. The California gray is the kind usually taken by the Indians, the others being but rarely attacked.

Their method of whaling, being both novel and interesting, will require a minute description—not only the implements used, but the mode of attack, and the final disposition of the whale, being entirely different from the practice of our own whalemen. The harpoon consists of a barbed head, to which is attached a rope or lanyard, always of the same length, about five fathoms or thirty feet. This lanyard is made of whale's sinews twisted into a rope about an inch and a half in circumference, and covered with twine wound around it very tightly, called by sailors "serving." The rope is exceedingly strong and very pliable.

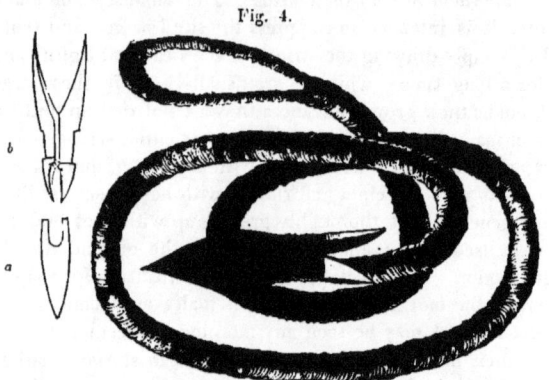

Fig. 4.

Harpoon point (kwe-káhptl) and line. a. Blade. b. Barbs.

The harpoon-head is a flat piece of iron or copper, usually a saw-blade or a piece of sheet copper, to which a couple of barbs made of elk's or deer's horn are secured, and the whole covered with a coating of spruce gum. The staff is made of yew in two pieces, which are joined in the middle by a very neat scarph, firmly secured by a narrow strip of bark wound around it very tightly. I do not know why these staves or handles are not made of one piece; it may be that the yew does not grow sufficiently straight to afford the required length; but I have never seen a staff that was not constructed as here described. The length is eighteen feet; thickest in the centre, where it is joined together, and tapering thence to both ends. To be used, the staff is inserted into the barbed head, and the end of the lanyard made fast to a buoy, which is simply a seal-skin taken from the animal whole, the hair being left inwards. The apertures of the head, feet, and tail are tied up airtight, and the skin inflated like a bladder.

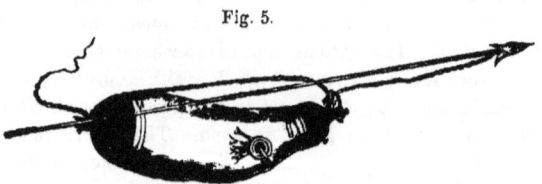

Fig. 5.

Seal skin buoy (Do-ko-kup-tl).

When the harpoon is driven into a whale the barb and buoy remain fastened to him, but the staff comes out, and is taken into the canoe. The harpoon which is thrown into the head of the whale has but one buoy attached; but those thrown into the body have as many as can be conveniently tied on; and, when a number of canoes join in the attack, it is not unusual for from thirty to forty of these buoys to be made fast to the whale, which, of course, cannot sink, and is easily despatched by their spears and lances. The buoys are fastened together by means of a stout line made of spruce roots, first slightly roasted in hot ashes, then split with knives into fine fibres, and finally twisted into ropes, which are very strong and durable. These ropes are also used for towing the dead whale to the shore. The harpoon-head is called kwe-kaptl; the barbs, tsa-kwat; the blade, kūt-só-wit; the lanyard attached to the head, klūks-ko; the loop at the end of the lanyard, kle-tait-lĭsh; the staff of the harpoon, du-pói-ak; the buoy, dōpt-kó-kuptl, and the buoy-rope, tsis-ka-pūb.

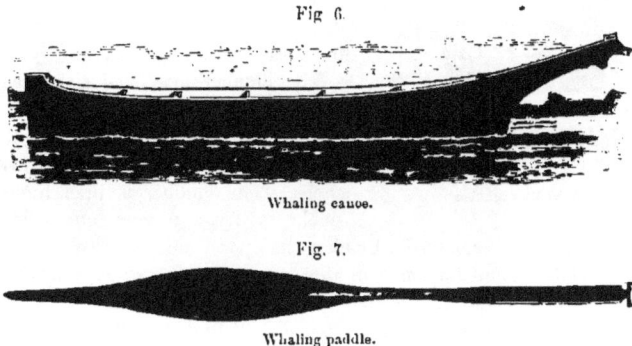

Fig 6.

Whaling canoe.

Fig. 7.

Whaling paddle.

A whaling canoe invariably carries eight men: one in the bow, who is the harpooner, one in the stern to steer, and six to paddle. The canoe is divided by sticks, which serve as stretchers or thwarts, into six spaces, named as follows: the bow, he-tuk-wad; the space immediately behind, ka-kai-woks; centre of canoe, cha-t'hluk-dōs; next space, he-stuk'-stas; stern, kli-chá. This canoe is called pa-dau-t'hl. A canoe that carries six persons, or one of medium size, is called bo-kwis'-tat; a smaller size, a-tlis-tat; and very small ones for fishing, te-ka-aú-da.

When whales are in sight, and one or more canoes have put off in pursuit, it is usual for some one to be on the look-out from a high position, so that in case a whale is struck, a signal can be given and other canoes go to assist. When the whale is dead, it is towed ashore to the most convenient spot, if possible to one of the villages, and hauled as high on the beach as it can be floated. As soon as the tide recedes, all hands swarm around the carcass with their knives, and in a very short time the blubber is stripped off in blocks about two feet square. The portion of blubber forming a saddle, taken from between the head and dorsal fin, is esteemed the most choice, and is always the property of the person who first strikes the whale. The other portions are distributed according to rule, each man knowing what he is to receive. The saddle is termed u-butsk. It is placed across a pole supported by two stout posts. At each end of the pole are hung the harpoons and lines with which the whale was killed. Next to the blubber at each end are the whale's eyes; eagle's feathers are stuck in a row along the top, a bunch of feathers at each end, and the whole covered over with spots and patches of down. Underneath the blubber is a trough to catch the oil which drips out. The u-butsk remains in a conspicuous part of the lodge until it is considered ripe enough to eat, when a feast is held, and the whole devoured or carried off by the guests, who are at liberty to carry away what they cannot eat. After the blubber is removed into the lodge the black skin is first taken off, and either eaten raw or else boiled. It looks like India rubber; but though very repulsive to the eye it is by no means unpalatable, and is usually given to the children, who are very fond of it, and manage to besmear their faces with the grease till they are in a filthy condition.

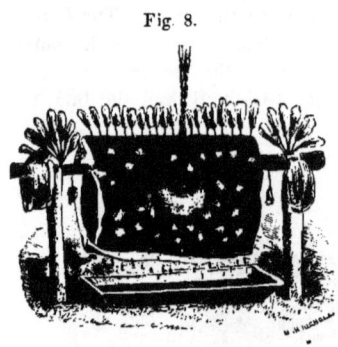

Fig. 8.

Saddle of whale's blubber.

The blubber, after being skinned, is cut into strips and boiled, to get out the oil that can be extracted by that process; this oil is carefully skimmed from the pots with clam shells. The blubber is then hung in the smoke to dry, and when cured, looks very much like citron. It is somewhat tougher than pork, but sweet (if the whale has been recently killed), and has none of that nauseous taste which the whites attribute to it. When cooked, it is common to boil the strips about twenty minutes; but it is often eaten cold and as an accompaniment to dried halibut.

From information I obtained, I infer that formerly the Indians were more successful in killing whales than they have been of late years. Whether the whales were more numerous, or that the Indians, being now able to procure other food from the whites, have become indifferent to the pursuit, I cannot say; but I have not noticed any marked activity among them, and when they do go out they rarely take a prize. They are more successful in their whaling in some seasons than in others, and whenever a surplus of oil or blubber is on hand, it is exchanged or traded with Indians of other tribes, who appear quite as fond of the luxury as the Makahs. The oil sold by these whalers to the white traders is dogfish oil, which is not eaten by this tribe, although the Clyoquot and Nootkan Indians use it with their food. There is no portion of a whale, except the vertebræ and offal, which is useless to the Indians. The blubber and flesh serve for food; the sinews are prepared and made into ropes, cords, and bowstrings; and the stomach and intestines are carefully sorted and inflated, and when dried are used to hold oil. Whale oil serves the same purpose with these Indians that butter does with civilized people; they dip their dried halibut into it while eating, and use it with bread, potatoes, and various kinds of berries. When fresh, it is by no means unpalatable; and it is only after being badly boiled, or by long exposure, that it becomes rancid, and as offensive to a white man's palate as the common lamp oil of the shops.

The product of the ocean next in importance for food is the halibut. These are taken in the waters of the strait in certain localities, but as the depth of water at the mouth of the strait is very great, the Indians prefer to fish on a bank or shoal some fifteen or twenty miles west from Tatooche light. The depth on the banks varies from twenty to thirty fathoms. The lines used in the halibut fishing are usually made of the stems of the gigantic kelp (*fucus gigantea*), and the hooks of splints of hemlock. A line attached to one of the arms of the hook holds it in a vertical position, as shown in Fig. 9. The bait used is the cuttlefish or squid (*octopus tuberculatus*), which is plentiful and is taken by the natives by means of barbed sticks, which they thrust under the rocks at low water, to draw the animal out and kill it by transfixing it with the stick. A portion of the squid is firmly attached to the hook, which is sunk by means of a stone to the bottom, the sinker keeping the hook nearly in a stationary position. To the upper portion of the line it is usual to attach bladders, which serve as buoys, and several are set at one time. When the fish is hooked, it pulls the bladder, but cannot draw it under water. The Indian, seeing the signal, paddles out; hauls up the line; knocks the fish on the head with a club; readjusts his bait; casts it overboard; and proceeds to the next bladder he sees giving token of a fish. When a number of Indians are together in a large canoe, and the fish bite readily, it is usual to fish from the canoe without using the buoy. This hook is called che-būd, and the club, sometimes fancifully carved, is called ti-ne-t'hl.

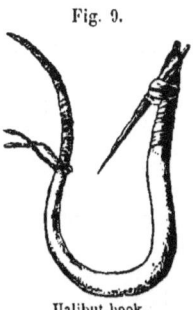

Fig. 9.

Halibut hook.

When the fish are brought home, they are first landed on the beach, where the women wash and wipe them with a wisp of grass or fern. The entrails are taken out and thrown away, and the rest of the fish carried into the houses. The heads are taken off first to be dried separately, and the body of the fish is sliced by means of a knife of peculiar construction, somewhat resembling a common chopping knife, called kó-che-tin (Fig. 10). The skin is first carefully removed, and the flesh then sliced as thin as possible to facilitate the drying; and when perfectly cured, the pieces are wrapped in the skin, carefully packed in baskets, and placed in a dry place. The heads, the back bones, to which some flesh adheres, and the tails, are all dried and packed away separately from the body pieces. When eaten, the skin, to which the principal portion of the fat or oil of the fish adheres, is simply warmed, or toasted over the coals, till it acquires crispness. The heads, tails, and back bones are boiled. The dried strips from the body are eaten without further cooking, being simply broken into small pieces, dipped in whale oil, and so chewed and swallowed. It requires a peculiar twist of the fingers and some practice to dip a piece of dry halibut into a bowl of oil and convey it to the mouth without letting the oil drop off, but the Indians, old and young, are very expert, and scarcely ever drop any between the mouth and the bowl. In former times, dried halibut was to these Indians in lieu of bread; oil in place of butter, and blubber instead of beef or pork. When potatoes were introduced, they formed a valuable addition to their food, and since the white men have become more numerous, the Indians

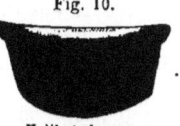

Fig. 10.

Halibut chopper.

have accustomed themselves to other articles of diet; flour, hard bread, rice, and beans are always acceptable to them; they are also very fond of molasses and sugar, and are willing at all times to barter their furs, oil, or fish for these commodities.

Next to the halibut are the salmon and codfish, and a species of fish called the "cultus" or bastard cod. These, however, are usually eaten fresh, except in seasons of great plenty, when the salmon is dried in the smoke. They are all taken with the hook, and the salmon fishing is most excellent sport. The bait used is herring, and unless these are plenty, they will not try to catch salmon, although the waters may be alive with them. A more extended notice of these fish and of several other varieties used for food, will be found in another portion of this paper.

The squid, which is used for bait in the halibut fishery, is also eaten. When first taken from the water it is a slimy jelly-like substance, of rather disgusting appearance, but when boiled it becomes firm and as white as the flesh of a lobster, which it somewhat resembles in taste, but is much tougher to masticate. I have found it, chopped with lettuce, an excellent ingredient in salad. The *onychoteuthis* is also found, but it is never eaten. Skates are abundant, but as they usually make their appearance during the halibut season, they are seldom used, although the Indians like them very well; but they seem to prefer halibut. Three varieties of *echinus* are found here, and are eaten in great quantities; they are either caught by spearing them at low tide, or are taken in a very simple manner by means of a piece of kelp. To effect this a stem of the kelp is sunk to the bottom, having a line and buoy attached. The echini go on it to feed, and after the kelp has remained several hours, it is gently drawn into a canoe and the creature picked off. The Indians collect them in this manner in great numbers during the spring months. Although a variety of bivalves is found, they do not abound as they do in the bays further up the Strait, and do not form a common article of nutriment, except that mussels of the finest description cover the rocks about Cape Flattery and Tatooche Island, and are eaten whenever the Indian appetite craves them, or when the breakers of the Pacific are sufficiently quiet to permit a search. These are either boiled or roasted in the ashes, and are very delicious cooked by either method. Barnacles, crabs, sea slugs, periwinkles, limpets, &c. furnish occasional repasts. Scallops, which are found in the bays of Fuca Strait, are excluded from their list of food. They are considered as having some peculiar powers belonging to them, and in consequence their shells are made use of as rattles to be used in their ceremonials. Oysters were formerly found in Neeah Bay, but have been destroyed by some cause of late years; the only evidence of their former existence being the shells which are thrown ashore by the waves. They are found in the various bays and inlets of Vancouver Island, but the Indians do not eat them. In fact there are but few of the animal products of the ocean but are considered edible, and serve to diversify the food. Of land animals they eat the flesh of the elk, deer, and bear; but, although these abound a short distance in the interior, the Indians very seldom hunt for them, and when they kill any, as they occasionally do, they are always ready to sell the flesh to the white residents in the bay, seeming to care more for the skin than the carcass. Smaller animals, such as raccoons, squirrels, and rabbits, are seldom if ever eaten by them, and are killed only for the sake of the skin. Of birds, however, they are very fond, particularly the sea fowl, which are most plentiful at times, and are taken in great numbers on foggy nights, by means of spears. A fire of pitch-wood is built on a platform at one end of the canoe, and by the glare of its light, which seems to blind or attract the birds, the Indian is enabled to get into the midst of a flock, and spear them at his leisure. On the return of a canoe from one of these nocturnal excursions, particularly in the fall, it is not unusual to find in it a collection of pelicans, loons, cormorants, ducks of various kinds, grebes, and divers of various sorts. These, after being picked, and very superficially cleaned, are thrown promiscuously into a kettle, boiled and served up as a feast.

The roots used for food are potatoes, which are raised in limited quantities; Kammas (*Scilla Fraseri*), which is procured from the tribes south (Kwilléyute and Kwinaiülts), and some from the Vancouver Island Indians; tubers of the equisetum; fern roots, and those of some species of meadow grass and water plants; the roots of several kinds of sea-weed, particularly eel grass, are also used. These and the equisetum root are eaten raw; the others are all cooked. In the spring the young sprouts of the salmon berry (*Rubus spectabilis*) and thumb berry (*Rubus odoratus*) are consumed in great quantities. They are very tender, have a slightly acid and astringent taste, and appear to serve as alteratives to the system, which has become loaded with humors from the winter's diet of dried fish and oil. The sprouts are sometimes cooked by being tied in bundles and steamed over hot stones. After the season of sprouts is over the berries commence. The salmon berry comes first and is ripe in June; it is followed by the other summer berries till autumn, when the sallal and cranberry appear and continue till November. It is customary, when an Indian has a surplus of food of any kind, to invite a number of friends and neighbors to share it, and as they seem very fond of these social gatherings, scarcely a day passes but some one will give a feast, sometimes to a few, or it may be to a great number of persons. It is this fondness for feasts which makes them so improvident, for when they have anything they never seem satisfied until it is all eaten up. If one man is more fortunate than his neighbors in procuring a supply, instead of preserving it for his own wants and those of his family, he must give a feast, and while his supplies last the others are content to live on his hospitality; when that is exhausted they will seek food for themselves.

The articles used for culinary purposes are, for the most part, pots, kettles, and pans, principally procured from the whites, at the trading post of the Hudson's Bay Company at Victoria. The ancient method of steaming or boiling is occasionally resorted to, particularly in cooking quantities of meat, fish, or roots, for a feast. Large bowls shaped like troughs, cut from alder logs, are partially filled with red hot stones, on which a few fern leaves or sea-weed are laid; then the food, whether fish or potatoes, or kammas, is placed on this, a bucket of water is thrown into the trough, and the whole quickly covered with mats and blankets and left to steam till the contents are cooked. When larger quantities of food are to be prepared, the same process is employed, with the exception that, instead of using wooden troughs, a shallow pit is made in the ground. Potatoes and fish take only half an hour's cooking; but some of the roots, particularly the kammas, require a constant heat for nearly two days.

Their method of serving up food is very primitive, and the same forms are observed by all. When a feast is to consist of a variety of dishes, such for instance as hard bread, potatoes, blubber, fish, &c., they proceed in this manner: after the guests are assembled, the women begin to knead flour, and prepare it in cakes to bake in the ashes, the men meanwhile heating stones red hot. When these are ready, they are transferred by means of tongs made of a split stick, to large wooden troughs, and potatoes laid on top of them. Some water is then thrown on the heap, and the whole quickly covered with mats and old blankets to retain the steam. The potatoes having been covered up, the cakes are next placed in the hot ashes to bake. The guests meanwhile are served with dried halibut and oil; each has his allowance set before him, and what he cannot eat he is expected to carry away. Dry fish and oil constitute the first course, and by the time that is finished the potatoes are steamed, and the bread is baked. The potatoes are served first, and are eaten with oil, the custom being to peel off the skins with the fingers, dip the potato in oil and bite off a piece, repeating the dipping at each mouthful. The potatoes disposed of, the bread is next served; or, if they have hard bread, that is offered instead of fresh. Molasses is preferred with the bread, but if they have none, oil is used instead. If any more provision is to be served, it is brought in

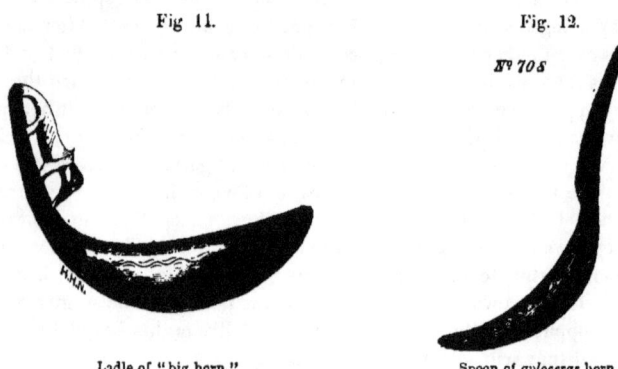

Fig. 11. Fig. 12.

Ladle of "big horn." Spoon of *aploceras* horn.

courses, and at the end of each course each guest wipes his mouth and fingers with a wisp of bark, puts whatever may be left into his basket, and looks out for the next course. The host is offended if his guests do not partake of everything that is set before them, and if strangers are among the visitors, it is not uncommon for four or five such feasts to be given in the course of a single day or evening, each arranged and conducted as described. I have attended several entertainments in visiting the different villages of the tribes. On one occasion, when an unusual display of hospitality was expected, one of the Indians who accompanied me remarked that I had better not eat too much at any one lodge, lest I should be sick, and not be able to feast at all of them, as I was expected to do. I asked him how he managed to eat such enormous quantities, for his appetite appeared insatiable. He replied, that when he had eaten too much he made it a practice, before going into the next lodge, to thrust his fingers down his throat, which enabled him to throw

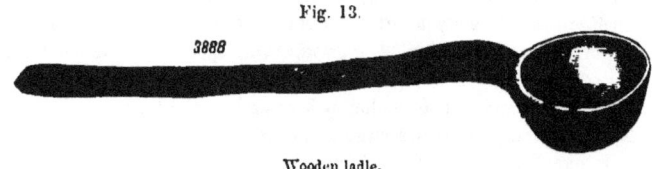

Wooden ladle.

off the load from his stomach, and prepare to do justice to the coming feast. An Indian who can perform this feat dexterously, so as to eat heartily at every house, is looked upon as a most welcome guest, who does justice to the hospitality of his host. Sometimes the feast is confined to boiled rice and molasses, of which they are very fond. This is served out in tin pans or wooden platters, and eaten with spoons made of horn, procured from the northern tribes, and said to be the horn of the mountain sheep.[1] If horn spoons are not at hand, they improvise an excellent substitute which is simply a clam shell, and with one of large size an Indian will swallow quite as much rice and molasses as by any other known method.

After eating, they sometimes, but not always, indulge in a whiff of tobacco; but smoking is not a universal practice among them, and is rather as a stimulant than a mere luxury; the pipe is more agreeable to them in their canoes, when tired with fishing or paddling; then the Indian likes to take out his little pouch of smoking materials, and draw a few whiffs. The article generally used is the dried leaves of the *Arctost uva-ursi* mixed with a little tobacco; they also use, when they have no *uva-ursi*, either the dried leaves of the sallal *Gaultheria shallon*, or dried alder bark. Smoking, however, is practised even less than among some of the tribes east of the Rocky Mountains, and there are no ceremonials connected with its use. Occasionally an Indian will swallow a quantity of the smoke, which, being retained a few seconds in the lungs or stomach, produces a species of stupefaction, lasting from five to ten minutes and then passing off. The calumet, or pipe of peace, with its gayly decorated stem, is quite unknown among these Indians. They are content with anything in the shape of a pipe, and seem to prefer a clay bowl, to which they affix a stem made of a dried branch of the *Rubus spectabilis*. They simply scrape off the bark and take out the pith, and the stem is finished. The smoking occupies but a few minutes of the time devoted to a meal; when they have finished, each guest gathers what provision he may have left, and all proceed to the next lodge, where another feast has been prepared; and when all is over, they return home with their gleanings.

OTTER, FISH, SEALS, &c., TAKEN BY THE MAKAHS.—Besides those already named, other varieties are taken, some of which are not used for food. As several have

---

[1] The ladles are made of wood, or of the horns of the "big-horn," *Ovis montana;* the spoons of those of the mountain goat, *Aploceras americana.*—G. G.

not been described in any work of reference I have seen, I shall have to describe them simply by their common and Indian names. The cottoids are very plenty and of several varieties, all of which are eaten. The largest, which is called tsá-daitch, measures twenty-seven inches in length. It is an uncouth, repulsive-looking fish, dark greenish-brown, the body larger in proportion to the head than other sculpins; but it is of good flavor, either boiled or fried. One specimen weighed ten pounds. The buffalo sculpin, kāb'-bis and other small varieties, are quite common, and are usually taken with spears. The kla-hap-pāk resembles the "grouper" of San Francisco. Its color is red; the scales large and coarse; the meat white, and in large flakes. It is excellent, either fried, boiled, or baked. The whites call it "rock cod," but it is not of the cod species, although the flavor and appearance of the flesh, when cooked, resemble that. The tsa-bá-hwa is much like the rock-cod of Massachusetts. It is variously marked, but the general color is olive-green on the back, shaded down to a yellow belly, and covered with reddish or brown spots or freckles; some are of a sepia-brown, with blue spots. It is a nice pan fish when fresh, but soon gets soft. Its flesh varies in color with the locality where it is taken, and the difference of food, and may be found with shades ranging from a pure white to a greenish-blue—the latter color being very disagreeable to most of the white men, who regard it as produced by a poisonous agency. I have eaten freely of this fish, and found that the color of the flesh made no difference either in flavor or quality. It can be taken by the hook while trolling for salmon, but is usually caught near the rocks with small hooks and lines. The cul-tus or "bastard cod," as it is termed by the whites, which abounds, and is taken at all seasons of the year, forms an important article for fresh consumption. This fish, in general appearance, somewhat resembles the true cod, but differs from it in many material respects. The dorsal fins are double, and extend from the head to the tail. These, as well as all the other fins, are thick, gelatinous, and palatable. This also differs from the common cod, in wanting the barbel under the lower jaw, which is longer than the upper, and in having both upper and lower jaws armed with strong teeth. The liver contains no oil, but the flesh has a portion of fat mixed through it. It is most excellent food, and especially when cooked, closely resembles the true cod. Exceedingly voracious also, in taking it the Indians use no hook; they simply secure a small fish, usually a perch or sculpin, to the line, and when the cod closes its jaws upon the bait, it holds with bulldog tenacity, and is hauled into the canoe and knocked on the head. The Indian name for it is tūsh-kaú. A fish closely resembling this, and perhaps of the same species, is sold in the San Francisco market under the name of cod. At certain seasons, particularly during the spring, it is found around the rocks and in coves of shallow water, and is then easily speared. The Indians seldom dry it, preferring to boil and eat it fresh. The true cod, ká-dátl, is taken in limited quantities. In some seasons it is more plentiful than at others. It is caught on banks and shoals, in from thirty to forty fathoms of water. This fish abounds in the more northern waters of the Pacific coast; but the extreme depth and swift currents of Fuca Strait make it difficult to fish for them there, except at those times during the summer months, when it approaches near the shore. Another fish, termed by the Indians be-shó-we, or black cod, although not a codfish, has not been described in any work that I have seen. It is a deep water fish, being caught in eighty fathoms. I have never been able to get one perfect. They are rarely taken, and those that I have seen had been split for curing. The color of the skin is black, and the flesh white and fat like mackerel. I have eaten some broiled, and the flavor was like that of halibut fins, extremely rich and fat. The weight varies from four to twelve pounds.

The dogfish (vá-cha) *Acanthias suckleyi*, is taken in great quantities for the sake of the oil contained in the liver, which forms the principal article of traffic between these Indians and the whites. Although this fish is plentiful on the coast south of Cape Flattery, I have never known the Indians there to make a business of fishing for them. Even at Kwilléyute, where I saw great quantities of dogfish in the summer of 1861, the Indians of that tribe and locality did not know how to extract the oil, and we had to send a Makah Indian, who was on board the vessel, ashore to show them how to try out the livers of a lot of fish we had caught.

The Indians on Vancouver Island, on the contrary, make a lucrative business of extracting the oil, and sell large quantities to the Makahs in exchange for whale oil, which they eat. The Clyoquots and Nootkans eat dogfish oil, but prefer whale oil when they can obtain it. The method of extracting as practised by the Makahs is to collect the livers, which are put into a tub and kept until a considerable quantity has accumulated. They are then put into iron pots, and set to simmer near the fire; or else hot stones are placed among them and they are cooked by the heat until all the oil is extracted, which is then carefully skimmed off and stored in receptacles, made of the paunches and intestines of whales, fish, or seals. In the fall of the year the flesh of the dogfish contains a considerable proportion of oil, which at other times it does not appear to possess; this is extracted in the following manner: When the livers are taken out, the head and back bone are also removed, and the rest of the body, being first slightly dried in the smoke, is steamed on hot stones till it is thoroughly cooked. It is then put into little baskets, made for the purpose, of soft cedar bark, and rolled and squeezed till all the liquid is extracted. This in color resembles dirty milk. It is boiled and allowed to cool and settle, and the oil is then skimmed off. After the oil is extracted, the flesh is washed in fresh water and again squeezed in the baskets, and in this state it is eaten by the Indians when other food is scarce. But dogfish is seldom tasted by the Makahs, and never until the oil has been thoroughly removed. The oil has a nauseous taste, and is not relished by these Indians, who are epicures in their way, and prefer the oil of whales and seals. The quality of dogfish oil for burning is very good, quite superior to whale oil. In astral lamps it burns with a clear, strong flame, and, when properly refined, is second only to sperm oil. Dr. Suckley states that while he was on service as surgeon at the U. S. military station at Fort Steilacoom, he used dogfish oil with great success in pulmonary affections, and considered it, when fresh, equal to cod-liver oil. A very large species of shark, known among whalemen as "bone shark," is occasionally killed by the Makahs, and its liver yields great quantities of oil. I saw one in October, 1862, killed in Neeah Bay, twenty-six feet long, and its liver yielded nearly seven barrels of oil, or over two hundred gallons. These sharks are very abundant during the summer and fall, but the Indians rarely attack them except when they come in shore to feed, which they do at certain times. They are easily seen by the long dorsal fin projecting above the water, and, as they appear to be quite sluggish in their movements, are readily killed with harpoons or lances. The flesh is never eaten.

A fish of the *Anarrhichthys* tribe is frequently killed during the summer months at low tide among the rocks. This is called the "doctor fish" by the Indians, and is never eaten except by some medicine-man who wishes to increase his skill in pharmacy.

Of the porpoise family there are three varieties in the waters of Fuca Strait. The large black kind called by the Makahs a-ikh-pet'hl; white fin porpoise, called kwak-watl, and the "puffing pig," tsailt'h-ko. These are killed with harpoons of a smaller size than those used for whales, and are highly esteemed as food.

Seals also abound. The sea-lion, the largest variety, is called á-ka-wad-dish; the fur-seal, kāt-hla-dōs, and the hair-seal, kās-chó-we. The skin of the hair-seal is always taken off whole, and, after the head and feet have been removed and the orifices firmly secured, it is blown full of air and dried with the hair side in. This is the buoy used for the whale fishery, and is usually painted on the outside with rude devices in red vermilion or ochre. The skins of the fur-seal are sold to the whites. The sea otter, ti-juk, is very rarely found around the cape, but is plentiful further down the coast in the vicinity of Point Grenville. During the summer of 1864 the fur-seals were more numerous in Fuca Strait than they had been for many years, and great numbers were taken by the Indians. Sometimes they kill seals with spears; but the common mode is to shoot them with guns. The flesh of all the species is eaten. There are several deep caverns in the cliffs at Cape Flattery in which the seals congregate during the breeding season. At such times the Indians go in with a torch and club, and kill numbers by knocking them on the head.

The ease with which these Indians can obtain their subsistence from the ocean makes them improvident in laying in supplies for winter use, except of halibut; for, on any day in the year when the weather will permit, they can procure, in a few hours, provisions enough to last them for several days.

TRADE.—The Makahs, from their peculiar locality, have been for many years the medium of conducting the traffic between the Columbia River and Coast tribes south of Cape Flattery, and the Indians north as far as Nootka. They are emphatically a trading, as well as a producing people; and in these respects are far superior to the Clallams and other tribes on Fuca Strait and Puget Sound. Before the white men came to this part of the country, and when the Indian population on the Pacific coast had not been reduced in numbers as it has been of late years, they traded largely with the Chinooks at the mouth of the Columbia, making excursions as far as the Kwinaiūlt tribe at Point Grenville, where they met the Chinook traders; and some of the more venturesome would even continue on to the Columbia, passing through the Chihalis country at Gray's Harbor and Shoalwater Bay. The Chinooks and Chihalis would in like manner come north as far as Cape Flattery; and these trading excursions were kept up pretty regularly, with only the interruption of occasional feuds and rivalries between the different tribes, when the intercourse would be suspended, or carried on by means of intermediate bands; for instance, the Chinooks would venture up as far as Chihalis, or perhaps Kwinaiūlt; they would go as far as the Kwilléyute, and these last in turn to Cape Flattery. After a while peace would be restored, and the long voyages again resumed. The Makahs took down canoes, oil, dried halibut, and hai-kwa, or dentalium shells. The large canoes were almost invariably made on Vancouver Island; for, although craft of this model are called "Chinook" canoes, very few in reality, except small ones, were made at Chinook, the cedar there not being of suitable size or quality for the largest sizes, and the best trees being found on the Island. The Makahs in return received sea-otter skins from Kwinaiūlt; vermilion or cinnabar from the Chinooks, which they in turn had procured from the more southern tribes of Oregon; and such articles of Indian value as might be manufactured or produced by the tribes living south of the cape. Their trade with the northern Indians was for dentalium, dried cedar bark for making mats, canoes, and dried salmon; paying for the same with dried halibut, blubber, and whale oil. Slaves also constituted an important article of traffic; they were purchased by the Makahs from the Vancouver Island Indians, and sold to the coast Indians south.

The northern Indians did not formerly, nor do they now, care to go further south on their trading excursions than Cape Flattery; and the Columbia River and other coast tribes seem to have extended their excursions no further north than that point. Isolated excursions are attributed to certain chiefs. Comcomly, for instance, the celebrated Chinook chief, would occasionally go north as far as Nootka; while Maquinna, Klállakum, and Tatooshátticus, of the Clyoquots, made visits to Chinook; but, as a general practice, the Makahs at Cape Flattery conducted the trade from north to south. In those early days, when so many more Indians were in every tribe than at present, and when they were so often at variance with each other, it is not probable that the trade conducted by the coast tribes was of any great value. But when the white traders began to settle at the mouth of the Columbia, the desire to obtain their goods, which had been awakened by the early fur traders at Nootka, caused a more active traffic to spring up, the Makahs wishing to get from Chinook the blankets, beads, brass kettles, and other commodities obtained at the trading post at Astoria. The entire supply was drawn from that settlement, until the Hudson's Bay Company established a trading post at Victoria, and, as trade could be conducted so much more readily at that place than at Astoria, the coast traffic was nearly stopped, or confined to the summer excursions of those Indians who had intermarried with the Kwinaiūlts or Chihalis. The coast trade south at present is confined to the exchange of a few canoes for the sea-otter skins of the Kwinaiūlts, but the amount is very small. Their trade with the Vancouver Island Indians is to exchange whale oil and dried halibut, for dog-fish oil, which is procured in large quantities by the Nittinat and Clyoquot tribes. The dog-fish oil is sold by the Makahs to the white traders. Formerly it went to those who traded with them at Neeah Bay; but of late years the greater portion is carried either to Victoria, or else to the different lumber mills on the Sound, where it finds a ready sale at prices averaging about fifty cents per gallon. They also trade off considerable quantities of dried halibut and whale oil to the Clallams and the Victoria Indians—receiving in return from these Indians blankets, guns, beads, &c., and from the whites either blankets, flour, hard bread, rice, and molasses, or money, which they usually expend before their return, in the purchase of those articles either at Victoria or at the villages on the Sound.

Blankets are the principal item of wealth, and the value of anything is fixed by the number of blankets it is worth. In the early days of the Hudson's Bay Company, and until within the past ten years, a blanket was considered equal in trade to five dollars; but since so many different traders have settled on the Sound, with such a variety of qualities and prices, the Indian in naming the number of blankets he expects to receive (as for a canoe), will state what kind he demands. Thus, if the price is to be twenty blankets, he will say, "how many large blue ones," which are the most costly, "how many red, and how many white ones?" and the purchaser must be acquainted with the value of the several kinds before he can tell what the canoe will really cost. Also in their trades among themselves they will pay for a slave, for instance, from one to two hundred blankets, but the number of each quality is always stated. They are very shrewd in their bargains, and from their long intercourse with the white traders are as well informed of the money-value of every commodity they wish to purchase, as most white people are.

I have no trustworthy statistics from which to derive information respecting the amount of their yearly barter; for, as I before remarked, only a portion of their oil is sold to the traders in the bay, the remainder being carried to Victoria, or the saw-mills; nor have I any means of ascertaining the value of the oil and dried fish they trade to other Indians I think, however, I am not far from the truth when I assert that their yearly produce of oil of all kinds will amount, on an average, to five thousand gallons. I have seen it stated in some reports of the Indian Department that the Makahs sold to the whites annually about sixteen thousand gallons of oil. They may possibly have done so in former years, but since my residence among them, I doubt if their sales have ever reached that amount. They, nevertheless, produce more than any other tribe I know of in the Territory, not of oil alone, but of the various products of the ocean; and were they a little more industrious, and more capable of realizing the advantage of taking care of their earnings, they would not only be a self-supporting tribe, completely independent of any assistance from the Government, but might actually become a wealthy community in the sense in which we employ the term. But they are, like all Indians, careless, indolent, and improvident, seeking only to obtain a temporary supply of food, or to get oil enough to purchase a superfluity of blankets, hard bread, rice, and molasses; and then have a big feast and give everything away. By judicious management on the part of the Government and its agents, these Indians might easily be taught to improve their fisheries of all kinds, so as to reap more lucrative returns; but as far as the Makahs are concerned, there are two very serious obstacles which will forever prevent them from being an agricultural people; and these two obstacles are soil and climate.

I have already shown that the whole of the reservation is a rocky, mountainous, forest-covered region, with no arable land except the low swamp and marsh, extending from Neeah Bay to Wäatch, and a small prairie at Tsuess. And not only are these lands too wet for the cultivation of anything but roots, but the climate is so exceedingly humid that cereals will not ripen. The only sure, repaying crop is potatoes. But Indians cannot live on potatoes alone, any more than the white men; they require animal food, and prefer the products of the ocean to the farina of the land. It will take many years, and cost the Government large sums of money to induce these savages to abandon their old habits of life and acquire new ones. In fact, these Coast Indians are an anomaly in their general style of living, as compared with the tribes of the plains, and as such, I think they should be encouraged in their fisheries, and taught to prepare fish for sale, to make barrels to hold their stock and oil, and helped, by means of the white men's experience, to take more whales and fish than they do now.

There is one article, and but one that I know of, which I think might be cultivated with profit, and that is the osier willow. If anything will grow in this wet climate, it appears to me it must be this, and, as these people are very expert in making baskets, they could easily be taught to manufacture an article from osiers suitable for our markets, or to prepare the osiers alone for sale to basket-makers. Agricultural labor is very odious to them all; still, a few will work, but they must be paid for everything they do. They are so accustomed to trade with white people and to receive gifts, that they will neither perform labor, however trivial, nor part with the least article of property, without exacting payment. They carried this practice so far as to demand compensation for allowing their children to attend the reservation school. They know the use and value of money, and are generally willing to do anything required of them if they can look for tangible results that will be of advantage to themselves. But they are profoundly indifferent to the benefits of education, and cannot be made to believe that clearing land, making roads, or draining swamps is of any use. When the season for planting arrives they are willing to put a few potatoes into the ground, because their experience has taught them that they can reasonably expect a harvest. But potatoes are esteemed by them rather as a luxury than as ordinary food, and, when they know how easily they can draw their subsistence from the ocean, and how much labor is required to till the earth, they prefer to continue in their old course, and let the white man's agriculture alone.

There are other articles of traffic, such as miniature canoes, baskets, mats, berries, &c.; but the principal source of wealth is oil and dried fish; the rest is only sold as the chance presents, on the arrival of strangers in the bay, or when they make their excursions up the Strait to the white settlements.

TOOLS.—The Makahs display considerable ingenuity in the manufacture of the knives, tools, and weapons they use, and are quite expert in forging a piece of iron with no greater heat than that of their ordinary fire, with a large stone for an anvil and a smaller one for a hammer. Their knives, which are employed either as weapons of defence or for cutting blubber or sticks, are made of rasps and files, which they procure at the saw-mills after they have been used in sharpening the mill-saws; or, not uncommonly, they purchase new ones of the traders in Victoria. They are first rudely fashioned with the stone hammer into the required shape, brought to an edge by means of files, and finely sharpened on stones; they are always two-edged, so as to be used as daggers. The handles are of bone riveted, and sometimes ornamented with inserted strips of brass or copper. As they are experienced in the use of heat, they are able to temper these knives very well. The chisels are made of rasps, or of any kind of steel that can be obtained. Sometimes they take an old axe, and, after excessive labor, succeed in filing it in two, so as to make as it were two narrow axes; these are then heated and forged into the required shape, and handles attached similar to that shown in Fig. 16. They are not all carved alike, but the mode of fastening the iron to the handle is the same. The instrument for boring holes in the canoes to receive nails or wooden pegs is simply an iron or steel wire flattened at the point and sharpened; this wire or gimlet is inserted into the end of a long stick which serves as a handle; and the manner of using it is to place the point of iron on the spot where a hole is required, and then roll the stick briskly between the palms of the hands.

Knives somewhat resembling a round-pointed cobbler's knife are also used, the end being bent into a hook. This tool is used in carving, or for work where a

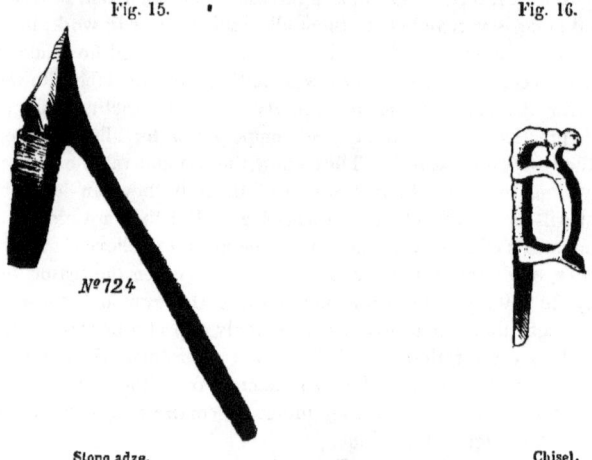

Fig. 15.　　Fig. 16.

Stone adze.　　Chisel.

gouge would be required, the workman invariably drawing the knife toward instead of thrusting it from him. All the native tools are made to operate on this principle. Cutting with a knife of any kind, or with a chisel, is done by working toward instead of from the person, and it is only when they get hold of an old plane that they work as white men do. They also make knife-blades from half an inch to two inches long, which are inserted into wooden handles, and used either for whittling or for scarifying their bodies during their medicine or ta-ma-na-was performances. Some of them have managed to procure hammers and cold chisels from the various wrecks that have been thrown on the coast from time to time; and the wreck of the steamer Southerner, in 1855, about 30 miles south of Cape Flattery, afforded a rich harvest of old iron and copper, as well as engineer's tools, which have been extensively distributed and used among the coast tribes of the vicinity. Those who have been so fortunate as to obtain iron hammers use them in preference to those made of stone; but they generally use a smooth stone like a cobbler's lap-stone for an anvil. The common hammer is simply a paving stone. They, however, make hammers, or, more properly speaking, pestles, with which to drive their wooden wedges in splitting fire wood or making boards. These pestles are shaped like that shown in Fig. 17. They are made of the hardest jade that can be procured, and are wrought into shape by the slow drudgery of striking them with a smaller fragment, which knocks off a little bit at each blow. Months are consumed in the process, and it is one of their superstitions that from first to last no woman must touch the materials, nor the work be done except at night, when the maker can toil in solitude unnoticed by others. If a woman should handle the pestle, it would break; or if other persons should look on while the work was in progress the stone would split or clip off. The night is preferred, because they imagine the stone is softer then than during the day. Any one can form an idea of the nature of this manufacture and its tedious labor by taking two nodules of flint or a couple of paving stones and attempting to reduce one of them to a required shape by striking them together. Yet these Indians not only fashion their hammers in this manner, but they make very nice jobs, and some that I have seen had quite a smooth surface with a degree of polish. They are valued, according to the hardness of the stone, at from one to three blankets.

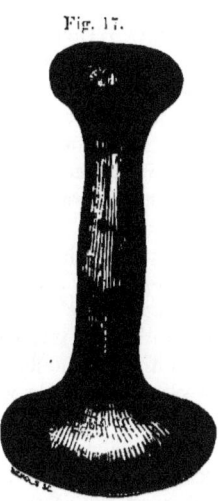

Fig. 17.

Stone hammer.

A canoe-maker's stock of tools is quite small, consisting only of an axe, a stone hammer, some wooden wedges, a chisel, a knife, and a gimlet. Those who are so fortunate as to possess a saw will use it occasionally; but the common method of cutting off a piece of wood or a board is with the axe or chisel. And yet with these simple and primitive tools they contrive to do all the carpenter work required.

The principal articles manufactured by the Makahs are canoes and whaling implements, conical hats, bark mats, fishing lines, fish-hooks, knives and daggers, bows and arrows, dog's hair blankets, feather capes, and various other articles which will hereafter be named and described. As I before remarked, the largest and best canoes are made by the Clyoquots and Nittinats on Vancouver Island; the cedar there being of a quality greatly superior to that found on or near Cape Flattery. Canoes of the medium and small sizes are made by the Makahs from cedar procured a short distance up the Strait or on the Tsuess River. After the tree is cut down and the bark stripped, the log is cut at the length required for the canoes, and the upper portion removed by splitting it off with wedges, until the greatest width is attained. The two ends are then rough-hewed to a tapering form and a portion of the inside dug out. The log is next turned over and properly shaped for a bottom, then turned back and more chopped from the inside, until enough has been removed from both inside and out to permit it to be easily handled, when it is slid into the water and taken to the lodge of the maker, where he finishes it at his leisure. In some cases they finish a canoe in the woods, but generally it is brought home as soon as they can haul it to the stream. Before the introduction of iron tools, the making of a canoe was a work of much difficulty. Their hatchets were made of stone, and their chisels of mussel shells ground to a sharp edge by rubbing them on a piece of sandstone. It required much time and extreme labor to cut down a large cedar, and it was only the chiefs who had a number of slaves at their disposal who attempted such large operations. Their method was to gather round a tree as many as could work, and these chipped away with their stone hatchets till the tree was literally gnawed down, after the fashion of beavers. Then to shape it and hollow it out was also a tedious job, and many a month would intervene between the times of commencing to fell the tree, and finishing the canoe. The implements they use at present are axes to do the rough-hewing, and chisels fitted to handles, as shown in Figure 15; these last are used like a cooper's adze, and remove the wood in small chips. The process of finishing is very slow. A white carpenter could smooth off the hull of a canoe with a plane, and do more in two hours than the Indian with his chisel can do in a week. The outside, when it is completed, serves as a guide for finishing the inside, the workman gauging the requisite thickness by placing one hand on the outside and the other on the inside and passing them over the work. He is guided in modelling by the eye, seldom if ever using a measure of any kind; and some are so expert in this that they make lines as true as the most skilful mechanic can. If the tree is not sufficiently thick to give the required width, they spring the top of the sides apart, in the middle of the canoes, by steaming the wood. The inside is filled with water which is heated by means of red hot stones, and a slow fire is made on the outside by rows of bark laid on the ground, a short distance off, but near enough to warm the cedar without burning it. This renders the wood very flexible in a short time, so that the sides can be opened from six to twelve inches. The canoe is now strengthened, and kept in form by sticks or stretchers, similar to a boat's thwarts. The ends of these stretchers are fastened with withes made from tapering cedar limbs, twisted, and used instead of cords, and the water is then emptied out; this process is not often employed, however, the log being usually sufficiently wide in the first instance. As the projections for the head and stern pieces cannot be cut from the log, they are carved from separate pieces and fastened on by means of withes and wooden pegs. A very neat and peculiar scarph is used in joining these pieces to the body of the canoe, and the parts are fitted together in a simple and effectual manner. First the scarph is made on the canoe; this is rubbed over with grease and charcoal; next the piece to be fitted is hewn as nearly like the scarph as the eye can guide, and applied to the part which has the grease on it. It is then removed, and the inequalities being at once discovered and chipped off with the chisel, the process is repeated until the whole of the scarph or the piece to be fitted is uniformly marked with the blackened grease. The joints are by this method perfectly matched, and so neat as to be water tight without any calking. The head and stern pieces being fastened on, the whole of the inside is then chipped over again, and the smaller and more indistinct the chisel marks are, the better the workmanship is considered. Until very recently it was the custom to ornament all canoes, except the small ones, with rows of the pearly valve of a species of sea-snail. These shells are procured in large quantities at Nittinat and Clyoquot, and formerly were in great demand as an article of traffic. They are inserted in the inside of the edge of the canoe by

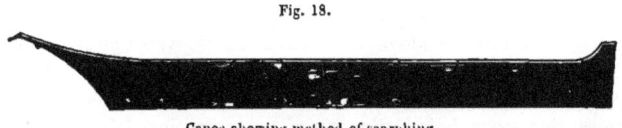

Fig. 18.

Canoe showing method of scarphing.

driving them into holes bored to receive them. But at present they are not much used by the Makahs, for the reason, I presume, that they are continually trading off their canoes, and find they bring quite as good a price without these ornaments as with them. I have noticed, however, among some of the Clallams, who are apt to keep a canoe much longer than the Makahs, that the shell ornaments are still used. When the canoe is finished it is painted inside with a mixture of oil and red ochre. Sometimes charcoal and oil are rubbed on the outside, but more commonly it is simply charred by means of long fagots of cedar splints, set on fire at one end like a torch, and held against the side of the canoe. The surface is then rubbed smooth with a wisp of grass or a branch of cedar twigs. When the bottom of the canoe gets foul from long use, it is dried and charred by the same process.

The small canoes sold to the white people as curiosities are made from alder; they vary in size, from two to three feet in length; but they are not good models of the great canoes, the head and stern pieces being too large in proportion to the whole, and generally the breadth is too great. Still they afford an idea of the general form. These miniature boats are usually painted in a fanciful style according to the taste of the maker. Some have in them grotesquely carved figures resembling men in various attitudes, but these do not really represent anything that may be recognized as a custom peculiar to canoe service. I have seen one with the effigy

Fig. 19.

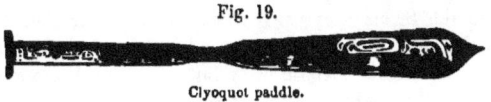

Clyoquot paddle.

of a man on horseback standing in it, a sight that of course was never seen. Not only are there no horses at Cape Flattery, but it is quite impossible for a man on horseback to get into, and stand in, one of these canoes. I have seen others with figures of owls, eagles, and bears in them. The Indians assured me they were merely fancy work, and I mention the fact lest any one seeing these rude carvings elsewhere, might be led to suppose that they were seriously designed to represent certain customs of the tribe. Neither the paintings nor carvings on these miniature canoes have any symbolical value or other significance attached to them. All the large canoes, in fact all except the miniature ones, are invariably painted red inside, and charred or painted black outside.

The paddles are made of yew, and are usually procured by barter with the Clyoquot Indians. The blade is broad like an oar blade, and the end rounded in an oval or lanceolate form. The handle is a separate piece fitted transversely with the length of the paddle, and sufficiently long to afford a good hold for the hand. These paddles when new are blackened by slightly charring them in the fire, and then rubbed smooth and slightly polished.

The sails were formerly made of mats of cedar bark, which are still used by some of the Clyoquots, although most of the tribes in the vicinity now use cotton. The usual form is square, with sticks at the top and bottom like a vessel's yards; a line passes through a hole in the top of the mast, rigged from the lower stick, and the sail is easily and quickly hoisted or lowered. When taken in it is rolled round the lower yard, and can be enlarged to its full size or reduced to adjust it to the force of the wind. Some Indians have adopted sprit-sails, but they are not in general use, nor are they as safe or convenient for the canoe as the square sail.

Fig. 20.

Canoe under sail.

In cruising on the Strait they usually keep well in shore, unless they intend to cross to the opposite side; and, if the canoe is large and heavily laden, they always anchor at night, and for this purpose use a large stone tied to a stout line. Sometimes they moor for the night by tying the canoe to the kelp. When the craft is not heavily burdened it is invariably hauled on the beach whenever the object is to encamp. If the wind is fair, or they have white men on board, they will travel all night, but on their trading excursions they usually encamp, which causes much delay in a journey. I have been seven days in the winter season making the passage between Neeah Bay and Port Townsend, about one hundred miles, and in the summer have made the same trip in but little over twenty-four hours. The average passage, however, is about three days for the distance named, which includes camping two nights.

WHALING AND FISHING GEAR.—This is a most interesting and important portion of the manufacture of the Makahs, and consists of harpoons, ropes, lines, buoys, fish-hooks, spears, &c.

The harpoon has been partly described before. Its head is made of sheet copper or sheet iron, cut as shown in Fig. 4, *a*. The barbs are of elk or deer horn, and shaped as shown in Fig. 4, *b*. These are fixed on each side of the blade or point, fitted tightly, and kept in place by cords or strips of bark. The whole is then covered with spruce gum, which is obtained by setting a fat pitch-knot by the fire, and catching the melted pitch in a shell placed beneath. It is then kneaded till it acquires the consistency of soft cobbler's wax, and is applied and distributed with the fingers. The whole blade and a portion of the barbs are covered with this pitch, which when cool is hard and smooth, and forms a tapering wedge-shaped spear-head. The pitch is then scraped from the edge of the blade, which is ground very sharp. The lanyard attached to the spear-head is made of the sinews of the whale, twisted into a rope and covered with twine. It is made fast to the head by unlaying the strands, fitting them around the barbs, and winding the cord and bark over them while fastening the barbs on. The fisherman is careful to have the lanyard securely fastened to the barbs, for on it depends the hold of the buoy on the whale. The blades, not being so securely fastened, frequently get loose after being imbedded in a whale for a long time, although some that were shown to me have been used for years.

This species of harpoon would scarcely be strong enough to bear the strain of a whale boat towing by it, as is the practice with our whalemen; but as they have only to bear the tension of the buoyancy of the float which is attached to the lanyard, they answer the double purpose of impeding the progress of the whale, so as to enable the Indian to kill it, and also of keeping the body from sinking after it is dead. The staff of the harpoon I have already described.

The method of making ropes and cords from sinews of the whale is as follows: The sinews, after being well dried, are separated into small fibres, and when ready for twisting resemble finely dressed flax. The threads are spun by twisting them between the palm of the hand and the naked thigh, and, as they are twisted, they are rolled up into balls. When unrolled for use they are twisted in the same manner by rolling them on the thigh. The strands are prepared from fine or coarse fibres, as the size of the cord or rope may require. Twine too is made by the process just described; but ropes are first made into strands, and these strands are twisted by hand and laid together with much hard work, which might be avoided by the use of the most primitive machinery of our rope factories. But the Makahs use nothing but their hands, and, although the work is slow and hard, yet they manufacture as handsome ropes as any of the "hand-laid" articles of the whites.

Ropes of greater size, such as are required for towing whales, are made of the tapering limbs of the cedar, first twisted like withes; and from the long fibrous roots of the spruce. These are first cut in lengths of three or four feet, and then subjected to a process of roasting or steaming in the ashes, which renders them extremely tough and pliable and easy to split. They are reduced to fine strands or threads with knives, and are then twisted and laid in ropes by the same process as that described for making the rope of sinews. Those that are attached to the buoys have one end very neatly tapered down, as shown in Fig. 4. This is to enable the whalemen to tie the rope with facility, and to pass it readily through the loop in the end of the harpoon lanyard. In making ropes, it is customary for quite a number of persons to assist. They are invited by the man who wishes to get ready his whaling gear, and each prepares a portion of the roots or sinews, so as to have as much as may be required at once. The next operation is to twist the fibres into threads. Another party, perhaps the same individuals, will meet on another day and work till the strands are completed. Then there may be a resting spell, probably because the provisions are exhausted and more must be obtained. The operation is often interrupted, and resumed at intervals, consequently much time is consumed in completing the work, a rope of thirty fathoms occupying frequently a whole winter in its manufacture.

Fishing lines, as already described, are made of the kelp stem. This is collected by means of two sticks joined like the letter y. At the bottom a stone is secured as a sinker; five or six inches above the stone a knife-blade is fastened between the two sticks, and a line is then fastened to the upper ends. This instrument is slipped over the bulb of kelp and lowered to the bottom, and a slight pull severs the stem close to the ground. They usually prefer the kelp growing in ten or twelve fathoms of water; most of the stems, however, that they procure rarely exceed ten fathoms in length, and many are not over five. The lower portion of the kelp stem is solid and cylindrical, and about a fourth of an inch in diameter. It retains this size for five or six fathoms, and then increases very gradually to the surface of the water, where it terminates in a globular head from four to six inches in diameter, from which float long streamer-like leaves. For more than half its length the stem is hollow, but this section is not taken for lines. The bulbs are frequently used to hold bait, or as water-bottles for fishermen. When a sufficient number of stems have been cut they are placed in fresh water—a running brook being always preferred—where they remain for five or six days, or until they become bleached nearly white. They are then partially dried in the smoke, and knotted together at the ends, and further dried in the sun, after being stretched to their full length, and to their utmost tension. This process reduces the size to that of a cod-line. They require several days' exposure to the sun and air before they are sufficiently cured They are taken in every night while curing, and are coiled up very neatly each time. When perfectly dry they are brittle, and break easily, but, when wet, they are exceedingly strong, fully equal to the best of hemp cod-lines. The usual length is from eighty to one hundred fathoms, although it is seldom that fishing is attempted at that depth, except for the "*be-shó-we*" or black cod; and the probable reason for their being so long is to guard against accidents by which a portion of the line may be lost. When fishing in shoal water, it is usual to untie a portion of the line at the required depth, and lay the remainder on one side, so as not to endanger its being entangled by the fish that may be caught.

Lines for small fish are made from kelp stems of the first year's growth, which are about as large as pipe-stems, with heads perfectly round and of the size of billiard balls. I supposed from the dissimilarity in the appearance of the kelp that it was a different variety, till the Indians assured me that it was all the same, but that it did not attain its full growth the first year. I have had no means of making observations to satisfy myself on this point; but as they make so much use of kelp, and seem to know so much about it, I am inclined to think they must be correct.

The halibut hook (Fig. 9) is a peculiarly shaped instrument, and is made of splints from hemlock knots bent in a form somewhat resembling an ox bow. These knots remain perfectly sound long after the body of the tree has decayed, and are exceedingly tough. They are selected in preference to those of spruce because there is no pitch in them to offend the fish, which will not bite at a hook that smells of resin. The knots are first split into small pieces, and after being shaped with a knife, are inserted into a hollow piece of the stem of the kelp and roasted or steamed in the hot ashes until they are pliable; they are then bent into the required form, and tied until they are cold, when they retain the shape given them. A barb made of a piece of bone is firmly lashed on the lower side of the hook with slips of spruce cut thin like a ribbon, or with strips of bark of the wild cherry. The upper arm of the hook is slightly curved outward, and wound around with bark to keep it from splitting. A thread made of whale sinews is usually fastened to the hook for the purpose of tying on the bait, and another of the same material loosely twisted, serves to fasten the hook to the kelp line. As the halibut's mouth is vertical, instead of horizontal like that of most other fish, it readily takes the hook, the upper portion of which passes outside and over the corner of the mouth, and acts as a sort of spring to fasten the barb into the fish's jaw. The Indians prefer this kind of hook for halibut fishing, although they can readily procure metal ones from the white traders. Smaller hooks for codfish are made of a single straight piece of wood from four to six inches long, with a bone barb lashed on in a manner similar to the barb of the halibut hook.

Fig. 21.

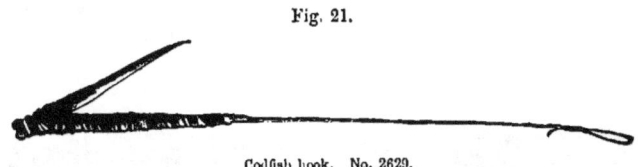

Codfish hook. No. 2629.

For very small fish, like perch or rock fish, they simply fasten a small piece of bone to a line of sinews. The bone is made sharp as a needle at both ends, and is tied in the middle. Many of the old men will not use any other than native made hooks and lines; while a few are very glad to obtain fish hooks and lines from the whites. In every canoe is a club for killing fish, which is usually nothing more than a billet of wood roughly fashioned, though sometimes rudely carved, as seen in

Figs. 22, 23. This club is about a foot long, and is commonly made of yew, and its use is to stun the fish by striking it on the head before the hook is removed

Fig. 22.

Fish club.

Fig. 23.

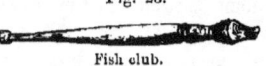

Fish club.

Fig. 24.

from the mouth. Another instrument used in fishing is called the kák-te-wahd'-de (Fig. 24). This is formed of two slender slips of cedar something in the shape of feathers. What would be the quill part is fastened to a bit of wood with a stone in it, to keep the instrument in an upright position. It is used for attracting fish when they do not bite readily. The Indian takes his fishing spear, thrusts the kák-te-wahd-de to the bottom, and when he releases it, its buoyancy brings it to the surface, while the wooden blades or feathers create a rotary or gyratory motion which attracts the fish.

BOXES, BASKETS, MATS, &c.—Vessels for carrying water, and large boxes for containing blankets or clothing, are made in the following manner: a board as wide as the box is intended to be high, is carefully smoothed with a chisel, then marked off into four divisions, and at each of the marks cut nearly in two. The wood is then wet with warm water, and gently bent around until the corners are fully formed. Thus three corners of the box are made, and the remaining one formed by the meeting of the two ends of the board, is fastened by wooden pegs. The bottom is then tightly fitted in by pins, and the box is made. The water box or bucket consists of one of these, and the chest is simply two large boxes, one shutting down over the other. These boxes are manufactured principally by the Clyoquot Indians, very few being made by the Makahs, on account of the scarcity of good cedar. They procure these by barter, and every lodge has a greater or less number of them according to the wealth of the occupants. Many have trunks purchased from the whites, either of Chinese or American manufacture, but although they can readily supply themselves at cheap rates with these as well as

Fig. 25. No. 2566.

Fig. 26.

with water pails, they prefer those used by their ancestors. Wooden bowls and dishes are usually manufactured from alder (Figs. 25 to 28). Some are of an oblong shape and used as chopping trays (Figs. 27 and 28). The wood of the alder, when freshly cut, is soft and white and easily worked, but a short exposure to the air

Fig. 27. No. 1137.

Wooden trencher.

Fig. 28.

Wooden bowls and dishes.

hardens and turns it to a red color. The bark chewed and spit into a dish forms a bright red dye pigment of a permanent color, which is used for dyeing cedar bark or grass. I have tried to extract this color by other means, but find that no process produces so good a dye as chewing. Alcohol gives an orange color, and boiling water, dark brown or black. I think, however, if it were macerated or ground in warm water, with, perhaps, the addition of certain salts, a very useful dye might be obtained.

Bowls are sometimes made of knots taken from decayed logs of maple or fir, as represented in Figs. 29 and 30.

Fig. 29.   Fig. 30.

Wooden bowls of maple or fir knots.

FEATHER AND DOG'S-HAIR BLANKETS.—Blankets are not only made of feathers, or rather down, and of dog's hair, but also of cedar bark. The method of manufacturing the first named is to select a bird that has plenty of down, and, first picking out all the feathers carefully, to skin it, and then dry the skin with the down on. When a sufficient number have been prepared they are slightly moistened, then cut into narrow strips, each one of which is twisted around a thread, leaving the down outside, which thus forms a round cord of down resembling a lady's fur boa. This is woven with twine and forms a compact, light, and very warm blanket. The hair blankets are made from the woolly covering of a species of dog of a yellowish-white color, which, after having been sheared off, is packed away with dry pulverized pipe clay, for the purpose of extracting the oil or grease. When a sufficient quantity has been obtained, and has remained long enough in the pipe clay, it is carefully picked over by hand, and beaten with a stick to knock out the dirt. It is then twisted on strong threads, and finally woven into a thick, strong, and heavy blanket. The pipe clay[1] is procured at Kwilléyute. The weaving process does not clean out all this substance, since its presence can be readily noticed at any time by shaking or beating the blanket. Bark blankets and capes are made from the inner bark of the cedar, dried and beaten into a fine mass of fibres, which are then spun into threads, and woven into the required forms, the edges of which are trimmed with fur. Very nice ones are also made by the Clyoquot Indians from the inner bark of the white pine, which is whiter and softer than cedar bark.

GAMBLING IMPLEMENTS.—Of these one form consists of disks made from the wood of a hazel which grows at Cape Flattery and vicinity. The shrub is from ten to fifteen feet high, and with limbs from two to three inches in diameter. The name in Makah is hul-li-á-ko-bupt, the disks hul-liák, and the game la-hul-lum. The game is common among all the Indians of this territory, and is called in the jargon la-hull. The disks are circular like checkers, about two inches in diameter, and the fourth of an inch thick; and are usually smoothed off and polished with care. They are first cut off transversely from the end of a stick which has been selected and properly prepared, then smoothed and polished, and marked on the outer edge with the color that designates their value. They are used in sets of ten, one of which is entirely black on the outer edge, another entirely white, and the rest of all degrees from black to white. Two persons play at the game, each having a mat before him, with the end next his opponent slightly raised, so that the disks cannot roll out of reach. Each player has ten disks which he covers with a quantity of the finely-beaten bark, and then separates the heap into two equal parts, shifting them rapidly on the mat from hand to hand. The opposing player guesses which heap contains the white or black, and on making his selection the disks are rolled down the mat, when each piece is separately seen. If he has guessed right, he wins; if not, he loses. Another game consists in passing a stick rapidly from hand to hand, and the object is to guess in which hand it may be. A third game, played by females, is with marked beaver teeth, which are thrown like dice. Four teeth are used; one side of each has marks, and the other is plain. If all four marked sides come up, or all four plain sides, the throw forms a double; if two marked and two plain ones come up, it is a single; uneven numbers lose. Both males and females are passionately fond of these games, and continue them for days, or until one or the other loses all that can be staked.

---

[1] Diatomaceous earth. (G. G.)

Mats, Baskets, Ornaments, &c.—Mats constitute one of the principal manufactures of the females during the winter months. With the Makahs, cedar bark is the only material used. Other tribes, who can obtain bulrushes and flags, make their mats of these plants, which, however, do not grow in the vicinity of Cape Flattery. Cedar bark, which constitutes an important item in their domestic economy, is prepared by first removing the outer bark from young trees, then peeling the inner bark off in long strips, which are dried in the sun, folded in a compact form, and used as articles of trade or barter. When wanted for use, if for making mats, the strips are split into strands varying from an eighth to a quarter of an inch in width, and as thick as stout wrapping-paper. These are then neatly woven together, so as to form a mat six feet long by three wide. Formerly mats were used as canoe sails, but at present they are employed for wrapping up blankets, for protecting the cargoes in canoes, and for sale to the whites, who use them as lining of rooms, or as floor coverings. Baskets for various uses are also made of this bark; but, as it is not very strong, those used for carrying burdens are made from spruce roots.

The bark is reduced to fine fibres by being broken across the edge of a paddle, and, when perfectly prepared in this way, is put to a variety of uses. It serves to make the beds of infants, for gun-wadding, as a substitute for towels, and for gambling in the game of la-hull. It is often dyed red with alder bark, and worn like a turban around the head during tamánawas performances. In the mat manufacture some is dyed black by soaking it in mud, and woven in as a sort of ornament around the edge, or as the dividing line across the centre. The Kwilléyute tribe manufacture very neat mats of a species of coarse grass, and excellent baskets from ash, which grows upon the banks of the river. These are common among the Makahs, being received in the way of trade.

Conical-shaped hats are made of spruce roots split into fine fibres, and plaited so as to be impervious to water. They are very ingeniously manufactured, and it requires some skill and experience to make one nicely. These hats are painted with rude devices on the outside, the colors being a black ground with red figures. The black is produced by grinding a piece of bituminous coal with salmon eggs, which have been chewed and spit on a stone; the red, by a mixture of vermilion and chewed salmon eggs. These eggs, after having been first dried, form a glutinous substance when chewed, which easily mixes with the colors, and forms a paint that dries readily and is very durable. The designs are drawn with brushes made of sticks, with the ends chewed. Some Indians, however, use brushes or pencils of human hair for these designs as well as those on the miniature canoes; but the most common brush is simply a stick. The process, with these rude implements, is very slow.

Fig. 31.

Conical hat.

Beside the conical hats worn by themselves, they have also, of late years, manufactured hats which they sell to the white men. These are shaped like the common straw hat, and are made of spruce roots, and, although rather heavy, are strong and durable. Some have designs of various kinds woven in them, while others are plain, the color being of a buff, somewhat resembling the Mexican wool hats. This color cannot be removed by bleaching, attempts for this purpose having been made in San Francisco and Victoria; but the experiment proved a failure. The color, however, is no objection, and is indeed rather preferred; the hats being more generally purchased as curiosities than as articles for wear. Within a few years past they have taken a fancy to cover with basket-work any bottles or vials they can obtain, and, as they do this sort of work very well, they find ready sale for it among the seekers after Indian curiosities.

During rainy weather they make use of capes worn over the shoulders while in the canoes. These are woven whole, with a single opening in the centre for the head to pass through, something like a *poncho*. They come down from the neck to the elbow, and are usually trimmed with fur around the edges. Some are woven from cedar bark, and others from strips of cloth or old blankets. They are warm, and impervious to water, and when an Indian has on one of these and his conical hat, his head and shoulders are well protected from wet. The rest of his body he seems to care little about, and he paddles round in his canoe with bare legs and arms, seemingly as indifferent to the rain or the water as a seal or an otter.

The baskets made by the Makahs are classed according to the material of which they are formed, and the uses to which they are put. The large ones, made of bark, which are used for holding dried fish, or blankets, are called klap-páirk. Carrying-baskets, worn on the back, with a strap around the forehead, are made of spruce roots or cedar twigs. They are woven quite open, and much larger at the top than at the bottom, the form tapering down in something of a wedge-shape. This enables them to carry loads with greater ease, as the weight is kept well up on the shoulders. These baskets are called bo-hé-vi. Small baskets are made of bark and grass, dyed of various colors. Some are woven with designs intended to represent birds or animals; others in simple checks of various patterns. Other small ones are of bark, and a species of eel grass that bleaches of a beautiful white. These small baskets are called pé-ko. The various colors are produced thus: black, by immersing the material in the salt-water mud, where it remains several weeks, usually during the summer months; a place being selected where the mud is rich with marine algæ, and emits a fetid smell, the sulphuretted hydrogen undoubtedly being the agent that imparts the color to the vegetable fibres of the bark or grass; red is procured from the alder bark by the process already described; yellow from the bark of the root of the Oregon grape (*Berberis*), which is boiled, and the grass immersed in it. Bark is not dyed yellow, that color only being imparted to beach grass, which is used for weaving into baskets, and around the edges of some kinds of mats as an ornament. Grass in its natural state, by contrast with the other colors, appears white; but a pure white is obtained from the eel grass, or sea weed, which is procured in the bay, and bleached in the sun.

Fig. 32.

Bark basket.

Their ornaments consist mainly of the head and ear decorations worn by young girls, and of pieces of variegated shell inserted in their noses and ears. The first are made of the *Dentalium*, which is procured by barter with the Nootkan and other Indians of Vancouver Island. The shape of these ornaments is shown in Fig. 3, the shells being run on strings separated by pieces of leather, and so arranged as to form a fillet to surround the head. The shells, in the ear ornaments, generally have their tapering or small end up. These last are usually finished off with a quantity of glass beads of various sizes, shapes, and colors. They are not, however, attached to the head ornament, as shown in the drawing, unless they are very heavy; but usually tied to the ear, which is pierced all round the edge with holes, into which the strings are inserted. When the ornaments are laid aside, these holes in the ear usually have a piece of twine tied in them, and sometimes brass buttons are attached to the twine. This head ornament is very pretty, and when a squaw is in full dress she has quite a picturesque appearance. The shell ornaments for the nose are made of the *Haliotis*, which is procured on Vancouver Island. The largest specimens I have seen came from the Cowitchan district, on the eastern side; smaller ones are found at Clyoquot and Nootka. The pieces worn in the nose are of various shapes, circular, oval, or triangular, and hang pendent by means of a string; others are cut in the form of rings, with a small opening on one side, so they can be inserted or removed at pleasure; the size varies from a dime to a quarter of a dollar. Some of the ear ornaments, however, and particularly those worn by children, are much larger—not unfrequently two inches square. These are fastened to the rim of the ear by strings; they are not very attractive ornaments, as they serve to give the wearer a very savage appearance. Bracelets are made of brass wire, bent to the form of the wrist; some are rudely ornamented by notches filed in them, but most of them are plain. Finger rings are manufactured out of silver coin by first beating it flat, and then cutting it into strips, which are bent into a circular form and smoothed. The ends are not joined together, probably from the fact that they do not understand the art of brazing; although among the Haida and Chimsyan tribes the art of working in precious metals has attained a considerable degree of perfection.

BOWS AND ARROWS, FISH, AND BIRD-SPEARS.—The bow is usually made from yew, and bent in the form shown in Fig. 33; but many are straight, simply acquiring a

Fig. 33.

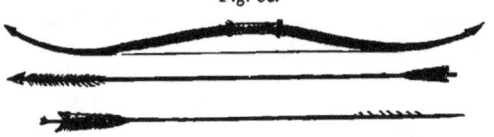

curved form when bent for use. Those that are made with care have usually a lock of hair fastened to the middle by means of a strip of bark wound around it. The string is made of whale sinews or seal gut, and is very strong. Inferior bows are made of a species of dog-wood which grows around Neeah Bay. This wood is white and tough, and also makes excellent hoops for barrels. The bow is used principally by the boys, who are not very dexterous in its use, but manage to kill birds and other small game; as a weapon of defence it is scarcely ever used, firearms entirely superseding it, most, if not all, of the men having guns. The arrows are made of cedar split into the required size and finished with a knife. It is usual when making arrows to be seated holding one end of the stick with the toes of the left foot, and the other end in the left hand, and to use the knife by drawing it towards the person. The arrow-heads are of various patterns; some are made of a piece of iron wire, which is usually obtained from the rim of some old tin pan or kettle; this is flattened at the point, sharpened, and a barb filed on one side, and driven into the end of the shaft; a strip of bark is wound around it to keep the wood from splitting. Some are made of bone with jagged edges, like barbs; others of two pieces of wood or bone so attached as to form a very acute angle to the shaft; others again are regularly shaped, double-barbed, and with triangular heads of iron or copper, of very neat workmanship. All the arrows are winged or tipped with feathers to give them a steady flight through the air. They are all buoyant, so as to be readily recovered after having been shot at waterfowl, for the aim while shooting from a canoe can no more be relied on than in throwing a stone. Frequently five or six arrows will be shot at a duck before it is hit, and they will often miss it altogether.

The bird spears are made of three or four prongs of different lengths, jagged, and barbed, and fastened to a pole or staff ten or twelve feet long, with a place at the upper end for the hand to press against. This spear is used at night, when the natives go in a canoe with fire to attract the birds. The prongs are made either of wood or bone. Fish spears have longer poles, and barbs of iron or bone, and are used for spearing fish, echini, and crabs. The manufacture of implements is practised by all; some, however, producing neater articles, are more employed in this way. The manufacture of whaling implements, particularly the staff of the harpoon and the harpoon head, is confined to individuals who dispose of them to the others. This is also the case with rope making; although all understand the process, some are peculiarly expert, and generally do the most of the work. Canoe making is another branch that is confined to certain persons who have more skill than others in forming the model and in finishing the work. Although they do not seem to have regular trades in these manufactures, yet the most expert principally confine themselves to certain branches. Some are quite skilful in working iron and copper, others in carving, or in painting; while others, again, are more expert in catching fish or killing whales.

Fig. 34.

Bird spear.

Although clay is found at Neeah Bay, the Indians do not know how to manufacture earthen or pottery ware. Their ancient utensils for boiling were simply wooden troughs, and the method of cooking in them being by hot stones, with which they could boil or steam whatever they desired to prepare. These troughs are used by many at the present day, and are preferred for cooking fish and potatoes to boiling in kettles; particularly on occasions of feasting, where a large quantity of food is to be prepared; but for ordinary purposes pots and kettles are used. Iron pots and brass kettles, with a goodly display of tin pans, are to be found in every lodge, all of which are purchased from the white traders.[1]

SONGS.—The songs of the Makahs are in great variety, and vary from that of the mother lulling her infant to sleep, to barbarous war cries and horribly discordant "medicine" refrains. Some of the tunes are sung in chorus, and many of the airs of the children do not sound badly when heard in the distance. They are good imitators, and readily learn the songs of the white men, particularly the popular negro melodies. Some of their best tunes are a mixture of our popular airs with notes of their own, and of these they sing several bars, and while one is expecting to hear them finish as they began, they will suddenly change into a barbarous discord. Their songs at ceremonials consist of a recitative and chorus, in which it would be difficult for any one to represent in musical characters the wild, savage sounds to which they gave utterance.

Some of the tribes sing the songs that have been composed by other tribes, and as they cannot always pronounce the words accurately, a person is liable to be misled as to the meaning. I was present, with several other white persons, at the opening ceremonies of the Clallams, at Port Townsend, a few years since. The chorus was a repetition of the words (as we all understood them) "a new-kushu ah yah yah." Kushu in the jargon means hog, and we supposed they were referring to that animal. The words, however, which they did pronounce were "wah-noo-koo-choo ah yah yah," but they said they did not know their meaning, they were "tamánawas." I subsequently ascertained that the song originated with the Clyoquots, and by them it is pronounced "wă-nă-kā-chee-ah yă yăh," and signifies a disposition to break things, or to kill their friends; and is in evidence of a bold and fearless spirit. Sometimes the young men assemble in the evening and sing some simple air in chorus, the words being generally improvised. They keep time with a drum or tambourine, which is simply a skin stretched tightly on a hoop. These songs sound very well, and are melodious when compared to some of their other chants. Many, both males and females, have good voices, and could be taught to sing, but their own native songs have nothing to recommend them to civilized ears. The words used are very few, seldom extending beyond those of a single sentence, and generally not more than one or two, which are repeated and sung by the hour. Sometimes they take the name of an individual, and repeat this over and over. A single instance will suffice as an illustration: There was a young Nittinat Indian, by the name of Bah-die, who was quite a favorite with the Makah boys. Some prank that he played caused his name to be frequently mentioned, and finally some one sang it to a tune with a rousing chorus. All the words used were "ah Bah-die," and this would be roared through all the changes in the gamut. This was a popular and favorite tune till Bah-die died, and then it was dropped, as they would not mention his name after he was dead.

---

[1] Arrow and spear-heads of stone seem not to have been used by the tribes in this part of the coast. Basket work and wood take the place of pottery, the manufacture of which article, however, again prevails among some of the tribes of Alaska.—G. G.

METHOD OF WARFARE.—The causes of feuds and hostilities between the coast tribes are usually of a trivial nature, generally originating in a theft, either of canoes, slaves, or blankets, or sometimes a dispute about a barter; but as these difficulties, no matter how they originate, are never confined to the principals, but are taken up by friends and relatives on both sides, reprisals are made on any one who may chance to fall in the way. For instance, a Makah visiting a neighboring tribe may perhaps steal something. He will not be pursued and the property taken away, but an opportunity will be embraced at some other time to steal from any Makah who may visit the same tribe. He in return may possibly kill some one, and then the whole tribe is held responsible. Sometimes several years may intervene between the commission of the first offence and the breaking out of hostilities; but every offence is remembered, and if not settled in an amicable manner, is avenged sooner or later. Since I have been among the Makahs, I have known but one war expedition, and a description of that will illustrate their general system of warfare.

An Indian belonging to the Makah tribe had a difficulty with an Elwha Indian belonging to a band of Clallams, who reside at the mouth of the Elwha River, emptying into the Strait of Fuca, near Port Angeles. The difficulty was about a squaw, and the ill-feeling had lasted for a year or two when the Elwha waylaid the Makah, and shot him. As the murdered man was a chief, the whole tribe were determined to avenge the murder; but first they referred the affair to the agents of the Indian Department, who promised that the murderer should be arrested and hung; nothing, however, was done about it, and at last the tribe, getting tired of waiting the action of the white men, concluded to settle the affair in their own way. After several meetings had been held, and the matter decided upon, they prepared themselves for war. The plan of approach to the Elwha village was first drawn on the sand, and the method of attack decided on. They then prepared great torches of dried pitch-wood made into fagots, and tied on the ends of poles. These were to set the houses of the Elwhas on fire. Knives were also sharpened, bows and arrows prepared, bullets cast, and guns cleaned. The largest canoes were put in war trim to convey the party, were blackened by burning fagots of cedar splints passed along under the bottom, freshly painted red in the inside, and decorated with branches of spruce limbs tied to the head and stern. There were twelve of these canoes, containing in all about eighty men, dressed with their blankets girt tight about the waist, in such a manner as to leave both arms free. Their faces were painted black, and their hair tied up in a club-knot behind, and bound round with sprigs of evergreen. They assembled on the beach previous to starting, where speeches were made and war dances performed; they then embarked precipitately and set off at the full speed of their boats up the Strait for Elwha village. As soon as they had gone, the women and children assembled on the roofs of the lodges and commenced a dismal chant, which they continued for a couple of hours, accompanying their music with beating the roof boards with sticks to mark the time. Each day, during the absence of the men, the women went through this performance at sunrise and sunset. On the third day the party returned, bringing with them the heads of two Elwhas they had killed. They came with songs of victory, with shouts, and firing volleys of musketry. When they had landed on the beach, they formed a circle, and having placed the two heads on the sand in the centre, they danced and howled around them like fiends. Speeches were then made, another volley fired, and the heads taken from village to village, at each of which the same scenes were repeated, until they finally arrived at Tsuess, the residence of the chief of the expedition, where they were stuck on two poles, and remained several months, presenting a weather-beaten and very ghastly appearance. From the parade the Indians made on starting, and after their return, one would be led to suppose that they had boldly attacked their enemies and burned their village; but such was not the fact. They crept along the coast, and after they had reached a point a few miles from Elwha, they hid themselves and sent a canoe to reconnoitre. This party discovered a couple of Elwhas fishing, and getting between them and the shore, killed them, cut off their heads, and returned to the main body, who, considering the murder of the chief fully avenged, returned without making any further demonstrations. Formerly, however, these battles were very sanguinary, numbers being killed on both sides and prisoners taken, who were invariably made slaves; but of late years they have confined themselves to occasional murders only, fearing lest any more extensive warfare would call down upon them the vengeance of the whites. They do not appear to have practised scalping, their custom being to cut off the heads of their enemies, which they bring home as trophies.

Since the system of reservations has been established, with officials residing upon them, there have been no attempts made by the Makahs to go on these war parties; but they refer all their grievances instead to their agent; they have, however, been threatened with an attack from some of the Vancouver Island Indians, and during the time the apprehension lasted they put themselves in a state of defence by erecting stockades of poles and brush about their houses, which they pierced with loopholes, and by keeping a constant watch night and day. Formerly they had stockade forts at Tatoosh Island, and on one of the rocky islets composing Flattery Rocks, where on an attack by their enemies, or during any alarm, they retired as to strongholds, in which they could easily defend themselves. These forts have been done away with for several years, and the only one that I know of at present, between the Columbia River and Cape Flattery, is at Kwilléyute. A precipitous rock, several hundred feet high, situated at the mouth of that river, is still fortified, and to all Indian attack is perfectly impregnable. I visited this rock a few years since, and found it several acres in extent on the surface, and with quite a growth of large spruce trees upon it, which are used both for firewood and for defence. There is but one path by which the summit can be gained, and to defend this they roll great logs to the brink of the descent, whence they can be easily thrown down on any force attacking them. As the approach is steep and slippery, nothing could prevent a log from sweeping down as many as might be in its path. The only way they could be subdued would be by siege and starvation; but that species of warfare does not seem to be practised among the coast tribes, their plan being to go in a body in their canoes, surprise their enemies, and return as soon as possible whether successful or not.

It has been customary to kill the men who fall into their hands, and to make slaves of the women and children; but very few if any slaves have been gained by the Makahs in this manner for several years past; all they have acquired being by purchase. They never bury their enemies slain in battle, as they have a superstition that the bodies would come to life again, and attack them; so they leave them exposed to the wolves; but the heads are stuck on poles, in order to be readily seen at all times. Thus, if the enemy should recover the bodies of his slain, and bury them, it would not matter so long as the heads were drying in the air. The two heads of the Elwhas that I have mentioned had remained on poles for several months, when the relatives requested permission to purchase them of the old chief who had them in charge, and offered ten blankets apiece; but the old savage refused the offer with the greatest disgust, and being fearful that I might possibly get hold of them for specimens, he hid them away in the woods, and I saw them no more. This chief, whose name was Kobétsi, or Kabátsat, was a powerful man, possessed of great strength and personal bravery. He was celebrated for his prowess in killing whales, and that, together with his being an hereditary chief, had given him the pre-eminence on all war parties. The other chief who headed the expedition was also a celebrated whale-killer named Häahtsc, or Sowsom.

GOVERNMENT.—Formerly the tribe had chiefs and head men whose word was law. The strongest man, who had the most friends or relatives, was the head chief, but of late years there has been no head. In every village there are several who claim a descent from chiefs of note, and call themselves chiefs and owners of the land, but their claims are seldom recognized, excepting that they are considered as belonging to the aristocracy, and are superior to the mis-che-mas or common people, or the köt-hlo or slaves. They are listened to in counsel, and always invited to feasts; are sure of a share of all presents, and of their proportion of any whales that are killed; but no one takes precedence of the rest, although many, if not all, would be very glad to be considered as the head chief provided the rest would consent. The eldest son of a chief succeeds to the title and property of the father, and in case of several children, of whom only one is a boy, he takes the property whether he is the eldest or youngest child. In case of a chief who died leaving one child, a son, the widow took for a second husband the brother of the one who died. By the last one she had a girl, and the father told me that his property too would descend to his brother's son, and not to the girl who was his own and only child. In the event of his having a son, the bulk of the property would still go to the nephew, whom he considered as his eldest son. The dignity of chief or head man can be attained by any one who possesses personal prowess, and who may be fortunate enough to accumulate property. An instance of this kind is in the case of Sekówt'hl, the head chief of the tribe, who was appointed such by Governor Stevens at the time of making the treaty. Sekówt'hl's mother was a slave, and his father a common person, but he was very brave and very successful in killing whales, and having accumulated much wealth in blankets, canoes, and slaves, was enabled to marry the daughter of a chief, by whom he had a son, who is also celebrated for his strength and bravery, and his success in the whale fishery, and is now considered as one of the principal chiefs of the village at Flattery Rocks, where both father and son reside.

THE INDIANS OF CAPE FLATTERY.

In the government of the tribe at present, all matters of importance are submitted to a council, which is held whenever any one gives a feast, or during the time of the ceremonials of the tamánawas. The old men on these occasions generally do all the talking, although women are permitted to speak on matters where they are concerned. I have known of but two or three instances where they have inflicted punishment, and on those occasions their mode was a pretty rough one. The first case was that of a man who was noted for his quarrelsome disposition; always in trouble, and always finding fault. Having become offended with his squaw, he turned her off and took another, a practice which is very common, both men and women leaving their partners on the most trivial occasions. Some time afterward the squaw got another husband, at which the first one was very indignant; and after much wordy warfare finally stabbed the new husband in the back. This was considered a gross outrage by the rest of the tribe; not the stabbing, but doing it without sufficient cause. The head men deliberated, and at last gathering together a band of friends, they proceeded to the village where the culprit resided, and after first securing him, they pulled out his hair and scarified the top of his head. The women finished the scene by pouring salt water on him, and rubbing his head with sand. One of the performers in this strange mode of punishment told me that the man felt very much ashamed, and would probably hereafter be more civil in his speech, and try and improve his fractious temper, a result very likely to be attained, as they promised upon a repetition of any more acts of violence to treat him to another and a severer dose. I have observed that he has been remarkably quiet in his deportment ever since. The other instances were for offences committed during the tamánawas ceremonies, and the punishment consisted in having sharp skewers of bone thrust through the fleshy part of the arms between the elbows and shoulders. After they had thus remained a short time, they were pulled out, and stuck in the bark head band, where they were obliged to be worn during the remainder of the ceremonies. In some instances they close the mouth by thrusting these skewers through the lips. This punishment is inflicted on those who laugh at or ridicule the ceremonials. In cases of theft, adultery, or murder, an opportunity is always offered to compromise the affair by restitution of the stolen property; and by the payment of a certain amount of blankets, guns, or canoes for the other offences; the amount of such payment being decided by the friends of the plaintiff in the case. If no such compromise is made, the aggrieved party will take his revenge either on the person who has committed the offence, or on any of his relatives; this revenge will be satisfied by breaking up a valuable canoe, taking forcible possession of any blankets or guns that may be had; or, if the offence consists in murder, by shooting or stabbing the offender or his nearest relative.

With the exceptions I have already noticed, there have been no instances, during my residence, of the tribe, or a number of them, being concerned in the punishment of offenders. All other cases that have come under my observation have been settled by individuals after their own fashion. In one instance a sort of bloodless duel was fought between two men, one of whom had stolen the other one's squaw. They were both slaves, and had the will to kill each other with knives, but the presence of the white men prevented resort to such extreme measures, and they were obliged to content themselves with seizing each other by the hair, and scuffling for a fall. After they had pulled one another about till they were tired, the victor, who in this instance was the man to whom the squaw really belonged, was considered entitled to her by the voice of the collected crowd. The affair was then considered satisfactorily settled. Others have been more serious. One young chief who had a grudge of long standing against another of equal rank, satisfied himself by shooting a brother of his adversary with a pistol, inflicting a serious though not a mortal wound. This affair, which caused much excitement, was finally compromised by the payment of certain articles. A common and favorite means of revenge consists in defacing or destroying canoes, and in other wanton acts of malice which would disgrace school boys; but as a general thing they have very few quarrels among themselves, compared with the breaches of the peace which so frequently occur in white settlements containing an equal number of individuals. This fact can be attributed to their freedom from the use of intoxicating liquor, which has been entirely prohibited on the reservation by the exertions of the agent. When, in former times, they had access to liquor, they were quite as quarrelsome as any other savages. Whenever a slave commits an offence, the owner administers punishment according to his own fancy, without consulting with others, or being held responsible for his acts. Two instances came within my knowledge where the slaves were killed. In one of these a slave went to Kwilléyute and murdered a man and woman, and on his return home was shot by his master. Peace was thus preserved between the two tribes, the murderer being rightly punished. In the other, a woman used abusive language toward her master, which he bore for a long time, till, finally, becoming exasperated, he struck her a blow on the head with a club, which stunned, but did not quite kill her. She remained in that state all night, and toward morning partially recovered; but the owner's wrath was not appeased, and he killed her with his knife. No notice was taken of this affair by the tribe. The owner, however, for this and several other crimes, was taken to Fort Steilacoom, and imprisoned for several months by order of the Indian agent. The Indians say, that formerly when slaves were more numerous, and more easily obtained, they were oftener punished. Instances are related in which an offender has been bound hand and foot, placed in a canoe and set adrift, while a strong east wind was blowing, which would carry him out to sea, and insure a miserable death by starvation. Others have been hung, and others tortured; but they are getting more moderate of late years, and extreme measures are seldom resorted to. The presence of white men has exerted a salutary influence in this respect, and the fear of being held responsible renders them more gentle in their deportment to their slaves.

The authority of the chief is respected relative to anything cast ashore by the tide, whether drift lumber, dead whales, or wrecks. Formerly, when each village contained but one head chief, he claimed and owned all the land between certain points, and everything cast ashore became his by right of seigniorage, and of this he could make distribution among his friends as he saw fit. The chief, for instance, who owned the land around Neeah Bay, was named Deeaht or Deeah, who, with his brother Obiee, claimed all the shore to the Hoko River, a distance of about eight miles. Decaht died without issue, and his brother Obiee or Odiee succeeded to his property, and his descendants still claim this right of seigniorage. The same custom prevails not only in all the villages of this tribe, but with every tribe on the coast; and as it is the custom, and agreed to by all, there is no dispute relative to any property acquired by jetsam. This right is not insisted on at present, except when a whale is cast ashore, or in case of wrecked property. Drift lumber, particularly mill logs, are so frequently brought down the straits, and cast ashore about the Cape, that any one who finds them has only to cut a notch in them with his axe, and his right is respected. The chief who receives any wrecked property invariably pays the finder something, or makes him a present of some kind. The chiefs also claimed the right to make prisoners of all who were cast ashore by shipwreck, whether Indians or white men; and, unless they could ransom themselves, they were detained as slaves. Hence we can readily account for, the avidity with which they possessed themselves of the persons and property of shipwrecked mariners who have from time to time been cast upon their shores. They looked upon everything thrown up by the waves as theirs, and it is but very recently that they have been led to respect the rights of white men, and to account to their agent for any wrecked materials coming into their possession. They still demand payment for anything they save, and, on the principle of salvage, such demands are just; but these claims are now arbitrated by the agent, instead of being left to the savages, as has always been the case heretofore.

HISTORY, TRADITIONS, ETC.—The history of this tribe, as far as their knowledge extends, is a confused mass of fables, legends, myths, and allegories. Nothing that they can state prior to the existence of a few generations back is clear or wholly to be relied upon. There are a few prominent events that have been remembered as having occurred; but the detail is confused, and it is very rare that two Indians tell the same story alike, unless it may be some wild and improbable legend, like the fairy tales related in nurseries, which are remembered in after life. A notable instance of this unreliability is in their version of the account of the Spanish settlement attempted at Neeah Bay by Lieut. Quimper, in 1792, by order of the commandant of the Spanish forces at Nootka. All they really know about it, is that they have been told by their fathers that the Spaniards were here, and they can point out the locality where yet may be found pieces of tile used by the Spaniards in building. But although that occurrence was only seventy-three years ago, there is but one man living in the tribe who remembers the circumstances, and he is in his dotage. Almost every Indian I have questioned upon the subject gives a different version of the detail. Now, as they cannot relate correctly matters given in our history, and of a comparatively recent date, but little dependence can be placed upon the tales of their origin, which are interesting only for their fabulous and superstitious nature. In the matter of the Spaniards, I have been told by one that they built a brick house with a shingle roof, and surrounded it with palisades. Another stated that the house was of wood, with a brick chimney; another that they built no house at all, but simply landed some bricks and other materials; and, before they could build the house, were driven away by the Indians. More recent events, such as the murder of the crews of the ship Boston, in 1803, and of the Tonquin, in 1811, and the captivity of Jewett among the Nootkans, they remember hearing about, and relate with tolerable accuracy. As events recede in years, however, they become obscured with legends and fables, so that the truth is exceedingly difficult to discover.

The legend respecting their own origin is, that they were created on the Cape. First, animals were produced, and from the union of some of these with a star which fell from heaven, came the first men, and from them sprang all the race of Nittinats, Clyoquots, and Makahs. Indians were also created on Vancouver Island at the same time. They claim for themselves and the Nittinats a greater antiquity than the Clyoquots or Nootkans, so-called, which were originally a mere band of the Nittinat tribe. The name Nootka, which was given by the first discoverers to the band of Indians called Mowitchat, or, as the Makahs pronounce it, Bo-wat-chat, has been most singularly accepted by all the authors; and not only is the tribe or band, and the Sound they live near, called Nootka, and the treaty of 1790, between Great Britain and Spain, relative to its possession, called the Nootka convention, but recent ethnologists class all these tribes as belonging to the Nootkan family. Had Captains Cook and Vancouver, and the early Spanish explorers made Neeah Bay their head quarters, there is no reason to doubt that the Makahs, or Classets, as they were called, would have been considered the parent stock, and the other coast tribes classed as of the Makah family. My own impression is that the Nittinats were originally the principal and most powerful tribe; and that the Clyoquot, Nootka, Ahosett, and other bands on the southwest portion of Vancouver Island, as well as the Makahs at Cape Flattery, were bands or offshoots from that tribe. We have seen that the name "Nootka" is not the name of any tribe on the northwest coast, but one given in mistake by the whites, and since adhered to. Still, it may perhaps be as well to class all these tribes as the Nootkan family, since that name has come into such general use; though there is no evidence that the tribe called Nootkas were the parent stock, nor can any proof of ancestry be obtained from any of the tribes, of which each claims an antiquity as great as the others.

There is, however, a marked similarity among all the coast tribes from the Columbia River to Nootka. But, farther north, the Haida, Stikine, Chimsyan, and other tribes are very different in appearance. This great dissimilarity can be noticed by the most casual observer in the streets of Victoria at any time. All these different tribes resort there for purposes of trade; and the northern Indians —for so those three are termed—can at a glance be distinguished from the Nootka family, or from the Flatheads. The northern Indians, so-called, are much taller, more robust, and with features more like the Tartar hordes of the Siberian coast. The women are much larger, better shaped, and with lighter complexions than the Flatheads, among which may be classed—of those who frequent Victoria, and with whom a comparison may be formed—the Cowitchins, Songish, Clallams, and the various tribes on Puget Sound, who all resemble the coast tribes in general appearance, manners, and customs. A northern Indian can as readily be distinguished and marked, among a crowd of Flatheads, as a Chinaman among white men. That the northern tribes have originated from wandering hordes from the Asiatic side of the Pacific, coming by way of the Aleutian Islands and Behring Strait, is in my opinion the most probable hypothesis, for there is as strong a resemblance to each other among all the Indians north of Vancouver Island, as far as Sitka, as there is among the so-called Nootkan family. Whether the Flatheads originally travelled by the same route, cannot be shown, either by their own traditions, or any other evidence that I have been able to get, during a very careful investigation among them, and the truth respecting their origin, if ever found, must be by evidence derived from other sources. The only tradition that I have heard respecting any migratory movement among the Makahs, is relative to a deluge or flood which occurred many years ago, but seems to have been local, and to have had no connection with the Noachic deluge which they know nothing about, as a casual visitor might suppose they did, on hearing them relate the story of their flood. This I give as stated to me by an intelligent chief; and the statement was repeated on different occasions by several others, with a slight variation in detail.

"A long time ago," said my informant, "but not at a very remote period, the water of the Pacific flowed through what is now the swamp and prairie between Wäatch village and Neeah Bay, making an island of Cape Flattery.. The water suddenly receded, leaving Neeah Bay perfectly dry. It was four days reaching its lowest ebb, and then rose again without any waves or breakers, till it had submerged the Cape, and in fact the whole country, excepting the tops of the mountains at Clyoquot. The water on its rise became very warm, and as it came up to the houses, those who had canoes put their effects into them, and floated off with the current, which set very strongly to the north. Some drifted one way, some another; and when the waters assumed their accustomed level, a portion of the tribe found themselves beyond Nootka, where their descendants now reside, and are known by the same name as the Makahs in Classet, or Kwenaitcheehat. Many canoes came down in the trees and were destroyed, and numerous lives were lost. The water was four days regaining its accustomed level."

The same tradition was related to me by the Kwilléyutes, who stated that a portion of that tribe made their way to the region in the vicinity of Port Townsend, where their descendants are known as the Chemakum tribe. I have also received the same tradition from the Chemakum Indians, who claim to have originally sprung from the Kwilléyutes. There is no doubt in my mind of the truth of this tradition. The Wäatch prairie shows conclusively that the water of the Pacific once flowed through it; and on cutting through the turf at any place between Neeah Bay and Wäatch, the whole substratum is found to be pure beach sand. In some places the turf is not more than a foot thick; at others the alluvial deposit is two or three feet.

As this portion of the country shows conclusive evidence of volcanic action, there is every reason to believe that there was a gradual depression and subsequent upheaval of the earth's crust, which made the waters rise and recede as the Indians stated. Fossil remains of whales are said by the Indians to be found around a lake near Clyoquot, which were possibly deposited at the time of this flood. I have not seen these remains, but I have been told of their existence by so many different Indians who professed to have seen them, that I think the story probably correct. The Indians do not think they got there by means of the flood, but that, as before stated, they are the remains of the feasts of the T'hlukloots, or thunder bird, who carried the whales there in his claws, and devoured them at his leisure. With the single exception of this legend of the flood, I have never learned from them that they have any tradition respecting the tribe coming to or going from the place where they now reside, and this is the only one which they relate of ancient times that is corroborated by geological or other evidence.[1]

The only genealogical record that has been related to me is one commencing twelve generations ago, beginning with Deeaht and his brother Obiee, or Odiee. This was told me by an old chief, named Kolchote, or Kalchote, who died two years ago. He was a very intelligent Indian, and held high rank among his people. According to his account he was a direct descendant, on his mother's side, from Odiee Deeaht (or, as it is sometimes pronounced, Deeahks, or Deeah, and by the Nittinats and Clyoquots Neeah), was the principal chief, and owned the land and resided at Neeah Bay, where Neeah village now stands. The bay takes its name from the village, and the village from its being the residence of, and owned by Deeah, who, dying without issue, was succeeded by his brother Odiee. His descendants were in the following order: Kat'hl-che-da, Wa-wa-tsoo-pa, Wat-lai-waih-kose, Kla-chetis-sub, How-é-sub, Ko-shah-sit, Tai-is-sub, Kloo-kwá-kay, Yáh-hie, and Kow-é-das. The daughter of Kow-é-das was the mother of Kalchote. Thus from Obiee to Kalchote are twelve generations. Some of the other Indians, who claim a descent on the male side, have told me that this story of Kalchote is incorrect, and that Neeah Bay was not named from Deeaht; but as they could assign no reason for the word, except that it was in use many years ago, I am inclined to think his version correct, particularly as he gave it to me just before his death, and it was interpreted to me on two different days by two different Indians, and was told me as an evidence that his only child, a daughter, was of high rank, and was to have his property, which he wished me to see distributed according to directions given at the time.[2]

The legend about Deeaht, and his tragical end, is as follows: The Nittinats came over with a mighty host and attacked the Makahs, driving them away from all their villages, and forcing them to retire to their strongholds at Flattery Rocks. Deeaht, who was a young man, very brave and influential, ventured back alone and built a house near the brook at Neeah village. He was shortly joined by his brother Obiee, and soon had a large number of friends and retainers around him. The Hosett Indians at Flattery Rocks, becoming jealous of his prosperity, came up and attacked him; but he defeated them and drove them back, discomfiting them so badly that they were glad to sue for peace, which he granted on condition of receiving for a wife the daughter of a chief residing at Hosett village. This

---

[1] Traditions of a deluge are also universal among the Flathead tribes, each claiming to have its particular Ararat.—G. G.
[2] The earlier names in this genealogy are probably of mythical personages.—G. G.

chief had a boy and girl who were twins, and could scarcely be told apart; so they dressed the boy in his sister's clothes, and delivered him to Decaht; but as soon as it became night the young savage, who had concealed a knife in his dress, cut Decaht's throat, and then made his escape to Hosett. Odice then succeeded his brother, and is the ancestor of a great portion of the Makahs who reside at Neeah Bay.

In one of the lodges at Neeah Bay are three carved figures, on whose heads rests the huge beam that supports the roof; of these one is intended to represent Decahks, or Decaht. Another figure, in the centre, is named Klessakady, and is symbolical of sunrise. His head is surmounted with a crescent-shaped cap, and between his feet is a head representing night. The beam above is marked with circular holes, to represent stars, and, according to Kalchote, the old chief, who placed it there, it may be said to show the manner in which the sun, when rising, thrusts the stars away with his head and tramples the night under his feet. A figure at the remote end of the lodge is named Billaksakut'hl, and represents a fabled giant of antiquity, who could spread his feet apart, leaving a space between his legs wide enough to pass the largest canoes through. These are the only carvings of any note in the village, but as to their significance, as stated to me by Kalchote, there is good reason to doubt its correctness. I recently asked the Indian who carved them, whose name is Dick, what *he* intended to represent? He said he had no other idea than to cut some posts to look like men, and that so far as the head between the feet of Klessakady was concerned, it simply meant nothing; but there happened to be a big knot in the wood, which made it difficult to carve, so he made a head of it; and after it was done, Kalchote painted it and set it up in his lodge with the other two, and gave them names, and invented the allegory himself. He explained himself further by remarking that he would carve me a figure if I would like, and that I could make any meaning to it I chose. Although Kalchote undoubtedly associated in his mind the allegories which he related to me with the images, the other Indians ridicule the idea, and say they are only Dick's work, which he did, with no particular object in view.

Each village has its own local traditions and genealogies, and each claims to have had, at former times, great men, who were head chiefs of the tribe. But it would appear that really each village was a community by itself, and they were often engaged in feuds among themselves; nor is this feeling wholly extinct; they speak of each other as they do of other tribes, and it is only on questions affecting the whole that they admit themselves to be all one. It is a common practice with all the chiefs of these tribes, Makahs, Nittinats, Clyoquots, Nootkans, etc., to claim great possessions, particularly when relating their tales to white men. Thus, if one's father or mother, or even the grandparents, belonged to another tribe, it is customary to claim the land of that tribe as theirs. For instance, one, whose mother was a Nittinat, will say: "That is my land at Nittinat." The chief of the Clyoquots, named Cédakanim, who frequently comes to Neeah Bay, told me that Cape Flattery was his land, because his mother was a Makah. His wife, who was the daughter of a Makah chief formerly residing at Neeah Bay, lays claim, in behalf of her son, to the land around the bay, as a portion of his grandfather's estate. Such claims, however, are ignored by the Makahs, or looked upon as merely complimentary titles. It was thus that the great chiefs of the Nootkans and Clyoquots made the early discoverers believe that they owned all the land south of Nootka and about Cape Flattery; and undoubtedly it was with this impression that Meares named the island at the entrance of the strait Tatoosh, supposing it to belong to Tatooshatticus, one of the Clyoquot or Nootkan chiefs. The Indian name of the island and village is Chahdi, and it is either called by that name, or Opa-jek-ta, meaning island—in the same manner as we would say, "We will go to Tatoosh," or "We will go to the island."

Taken in connection with the allegory of the thunder bird, Tatoosh or Tootootsh, which is the Clyoquot name of the thunder bird, seems singularly appropriate. The roaring of the waves reverberating in the caverns of the island, reminding them of thunder, and the bright flashes from the thunder cloud of the Ha-hék-to-ak—the producer of fire. But however amusing such an application of the name might appear, it has no foundation in reality, as the Indians do not, nor have they ever called the island by any other name than Chahdi. It is worthy of remark at this place that Maquinna or Maquilla, the great Nootkan chief mentioned by Vancouver, Meares, and others, is claimed by Cedakanim to have been a Clyoquot; while Kwistoh, a very intelligent chief among the Nittinats, has assured me that he was a Nittinat, who resided at Mowatchat, or Nootka. It is from conversation with these chiefs, as well as the Makahs, that I have formed the opinion that the Nittinat tribe was in reality the parent stock, and that the Indians of the southwestern portion of Vancouver Island, and at Cape Flattery, should be termed the Nittinat family, instead of the Nootkan or Clyoquot. I have not been able to prepare vocabularies of all these tribes, but their language, so far as I can judge from hearing them speak, is sufficiently alike to be recognized, and to leave no doubt that it was originally the same in all.

The changes that have been introduced among the Makahs by intercourse with the whites, can be summed up in a few words. Formerly they were clothed in robes of furs or skins, or with blankets made from cedar bark, dog's-hair, or bird skins; their weapons consisted of bows and arrows, spears, and stone-knives, and hatchets. Their food was the product of the ocean, the roots and berries indigenous to the Cape, and such wild animals and birds as they could destroy. Their trade was confined to barter among themselves, or the tribes of the coast. They were almost constantly at variance with other tribes, and lived in a state of fear and apprehension. They were cruel, ferocious, and treacherous, particularly to any so unfortunate as to be thrown among them, either by the fortunes of war, or otherwise. With the advent of white men blankets were substituted for their robes of skins and bark, and calico used for the simple cincture of bark worn about the loins; guns and knives were substituted for bows and spears; and potatoes, flour, bread, with other articles of food, replaced in a measure their fish, game, and roots. They acquired the knowledge of trade, and learned the value of money; but farther than this their progress has been slow. They have learned enough during their intercourse with the whites to make them careful about committing hostilities, knowing that the good-will of the white men, and the benefits of their trade, were means of enriching themselves and procuring many comforts; but their savage natures

THE INDIANS OF CAPE FLATTERY. 61

have never changed; they are as wild and treacherous as ever; and, but for the fear of punishment and the love of gain, would exterminate every settler that attempted to make his residence among them. Frequently, since the establishment of the reservation, they have made threats of hostilities; but the councils of those who desired to acquire property or hoped for favors have prevailed, and they have contented themselves with simple threats. Improvement in their customs, and habits, must be gradual, and the work of time and patient perseverance on the part of those delegated by the Government to reside among them and look after their welfare. They have steadily opposed everything that has been done or attempted for their benefit, and even now, though they see that the promises made to them by their agent have been, in great part, realized, they are totally indifferent as to whether anything more is to be done, and in no case volunteer a helping hand. Their ancient history is wrapped in an impenetrable obscurity—that of a more recent date I have endeavored to exhibit; their future can be read in the annals of the New England emigrants. The steady wave setting to our western shores will have its due effect upon the Indian races, and in the lapse of another century the places that now know them will know them no more.

MYTHOLOGY.—The Makahs believe in a Supreme Being, who is termed by them Cha-batt-a Ha-tartstl, or Ha-tartstl Cha-batt-a, the Great Chief who resides above. The name of this Great Chief, or Divine Being, is never given, although they have a name; but they must not speak it to any except those who have been initiated into their secret rites and ceremonies. They have no outward forms of religion, but each one addresses the Supreme Being by himself, and generally retires to the depth of the woods, or some cave, for the purpose. Intermediate spirits, or familiars, are supposed to guard the destinies of individuals, and to manifest themselves at certain times by visions, signs, and dreams. These are called in the jargon Tamánawas, and the receiving of a revelation is termed "seeing the Tamánawas."[1] I never with certainty have known an Indian to address himself to the Supreme Being until recently, while in a canoe with a chief named Klaplanhic, or Captain John. He was taken with a violent fit of sneezing, and as soon as he recovered he repeated aloud several short sentences, accompanying each with a blowing noise from his mouth. I asked him what he was saying? He replied that he was asking the Ha-tartstl Cha-batt-a not to kill him by sneezing, but to let him live longer. I have on other occasions, however, noticed that the Indians, upon sneezing, repeat a few words, and think it very probable they all do as John said he did—ask the Great Spirit not to kill them. John told me that, if they did not utter this brief petition, the top of their heads would be blown off when they sneezed.[2] The same chief informed me, during a recent conversation

---

[1] This word, which in Chinook means the practice of shamanism, in the jargon of the coast embraces everything supernatural.—G. G.

[2] A similar custom existed among the Peruvians, and runs through nearly all modern Europe. For the antiquity and universality of some superstition connected with sneezing, v. Encycl. Brit. also Encycl. Metrop., and Rees' Encycl.—G. G.

respecting their religious belief, that they think the sun is the representative of the Great Spirit, and to him they make their secret prayer. He also said that "The Indian Sunday is not one day, like your Sunday, but it is many days. When we want to talk with the Great Chief, we wait till the moon is full, and then go into the mountain, and rub our bodies with cedar twigs, after having first washed them clean. The cedar makes us smell sweet, and that the Great Chief likes. We watch for the sun, and when he first makes his appearance, we ask him to let us live long, to be strong to defend ourselves or attack our enemies, to be successful in our fisheries, or in the pursuit of game; and to give us everything we want. Every night we wash and rub ourselves with cedar, and every morning talk to the Great Chief, or his representative, the sun, whose name is Klé-sea-kark-tl."[1] We continue praying daily for one week, or from full moon to the quarter. The only instruction the children have as to the Supreme Being, or rather the only form of address taught them, is during the same period, when they are waked up at daylight and made to wash themselves before sunrise, and to ask the sun to let them live. Their tamánawas ceremonies are in reference to events they believe to have happened on the earth, and they try to represent them. But the doings of the Great Supreme they do not dare to attempt to represent, and only address him in private and at stated times. Their prayer is simply a selfish petition; they do not ask to be made wiser or better, but simply for long life, and strength, and skill, and cunning, so that they may be able to enrich themselves and obtain an ascendancy over their fellow-men.

At certain periods, generally during the winter months, they have ceremonies, or mystical performances, of which there are three distinct kinds. The Dukwally, or black tamánawas; the Tsiárk, or medicine tamánawas, and the Döt'hlub. The latter is seldom performed, the great variety of scenes to be enacted requiring a large number of persons, and a much greater expense on the part of the individual who gives them. All these ceremonies are commenced in secret, none but the initiated being allowed to be present; and it is then, if ever, that they make common supplication to the Deity. Although I have never been able to ascertain the real facts in the case, it would seem that they address themselves to some intermediate being. Certain other ceremonies are performed in public, and spectators admitted. From those that I have seen, I infer that the Dukwally is a ceremonial to propitiate the T'hlŭkloots, or thunder bird, who seems with the Makahs to take precedence over all other mythological beings. Into all these mysteries persons of both sexes, and even children, are initiated; but the initiation does not endow them with medicine or tamánawas qualities until they have gone through the private ordeal, of finding their own tamánawas, or guardian

---

[1] Among the western Selish, or Flathead tribes of the Sound, I have not detected any direct worship of the sun, though he forms one of their mythological characters. He is by them represented as the younger brother of the moon. According to Father Mengarini he is, however, the principal object of worship among the Flatheads of the Rocky Mountains, or Selish proper, as well as by the Blackfeet. Among both the tribes mentioned he was supposed to be the creation of a superior being.—G. G.

spirit. At such times they are supposed to receive some manifestation which guides them in their after life. This ceremony is performed as follows: The candidate retires to some place of concealment near the salt water, where he bathes himself, remaining till he is pretty well chilled; then returns to his hiding place, and warms himself by rubbing his body and limbs with bark or cedar twigs, and again returns to the water; keeping up this alternate bathing and friction day and night, without eating, and with no interval of sleep. Both body and mind becoming thus exhausted, he lies down in a sort of trance, during which, in his disordered fancy, he sees visions and receives revelations. What he sees he makes known to no one, but ever after addresses himself in secret to that being that has presented itself to him, whether in form of bird, beast, or fish, though the animal representing this guardian spirit is sometimes indicated by carvings or paintings made by the Indian. Such animals as would be most likely to come around him while thus alone are owls, wolves, minks, and mice, during the night; or eagles, crows, ravens, blue-jays, cranes, elk, deer, or seals, during the day. These are all considered tamánawas animals, some possessing more powerful influence than others; and, as an Indian could scarcely be several days or nights without seeing something of the kind, their ceremonies are generally successful in obtaining a manifestation. They do not imagine, however, that the animal they may see is the Guardian Spirit, but only the form in which he shows himself. Of the above, owls, bears, and wolves seem to be those most generally seen, and heads of these are more frequently carved than any others.

To illustrate their superstitious belief in animals connected with their Guardian Spirit, I will relate an incident told me by Captain John, one of the chiefs. About three years ago he had lost the use of one of his feet, probably from paralysis, but which he attributed to a "skookoom," or evil spirit, entering into it one day while he was bathing. He had been confined to his house for several months, and was reduced to a skeleton. I saw him during this sickness, and thought he could not recover. One pleasant day, however, according to his account, he managed to crawl to a brook near his house, and, while bathing, heard a rustling sound in the air, at which he became frightened, and covered his face with his blanket, whereupon a raven alighted within a few feet of him and uttered a hoarse croak. He then peeped through a corner of his blanket, and saw the raven with its head erect, its feathers bristled, and a great swelling in its throat. After two or three unsuccessful efforts, it finally threw up a piece of bone about three inches long, then uttering another croak it flew away. Remaining quiet a few minutes, till he was satisfied that the raven had gone, he picked up the bone, which he gravely informed me was of the Ha-hék-to-ak. He hid this bone near by, and returned to his lodge, and, after relating the occurrence, was informed by the Indian doctors that it was a medicine sent to him by his tamánawas, and this proved to be true, as he entirely recovered in three days. I knew that this man had recovered very speedily, but do not know the actual cause. He says he shall keep the bone hid till his son is old enough to kill whales, when he will give it to him to take in his canoe, as a powerful medicine to insure success. The tale of the raven alighting near him is not improbable, as ravens as well as crows are very plenty and very tame; nor is it impossible that the raven might have had a bone in its mouth, and finally dropped it; nor is it entirely uncertain that the circumstance so affected his superstitious imagination that it caused a reaction in his system, and promoted his recovery. The same effect might perhaps have been produced by a smart shock from a galvanic battery. It is thus, without doubt, that the persons going through the ordeal of becoming tamánawas, or medicine men, have their minds excited by any animal they may see, or even by the creaking of a limb in the forest, and their imaginations are sufficiently fertile to add to natural causes, fancies that appear to them to be real. If there is anything connected with their ceremonials approaching to our ideas of worship, it must be during the secret portion, from which all except the initiated are rigorously excluded ; but I have no evidence that such is the fact, and believe, as the Indians state to me, that the only time they address the Supreme Being is by themselves and in secret.

As their general tamánawas ceremonies are based upon their mythological fables, it will perhaps be well first to relate some of those legends before describing their public performances.

The Makahs believe in a transmigration of souls;[1] that every living thing, even trees, and all sorts of birds and fishes as well as animals, were formerly Indians who for their bad conduct were transformed into the shapes in which they now appear. These ancient Indians, said my informant, were so very bad, that at length two men, brothers of the sun and moon, who are termed Ho-hó-e-ap-béss or the "men who changed things"—came on earth and made the transformations. The seal was a very bad, thieving Indian, for which reason his arms were shortened, and his legs tied so that only his feet could move, and he was cast into the sea and told to catch fish for his food. The mink, Kwahtie, was a great liar, but a very shrewd Indian, full of rascalities which he practised on every one, and many are the tales told of his acts. His mother was the blue-jay, Kwish-kwishee. Once, while Kwahtie was making an arrow, his mother directed him to get some water, but he refused until he should have finished his work. His mother told him to make haste, for she felt that she was turning into a bird. While she was talking she turned into a blue jay and flew into a bush. Kwahtie tried to shoot her, but his arrow passed behind her neck, glancing over the top of her head, ruffling up the feathers, as they have always remained in the head of the blue-jay. Those Indians that were turned into wolves formerly resided at Clallam Bay. One day their chief Chu-chu-hu-uks-t'hl, came to Kwahtie's house, who pretended to be sick, and invited the wolf to come in and take a nap. This he did, as he was quite tired. When he was fast asleep Kwahtie got up and with a sharp mussel shell cut the wolf's throat and buried him in the sand. Two days after this a deputation of the wolf tribe came to look for their chief. "I have not seen him," said Kwahtie. "I am sick and have not left my house." The wolves retired; and shortly another, and then another deputation came. To all of these he gave the same answer. At last one of the

---

[1] The term "transmigration of souls" is not strictly correct. The idea is that the pre-human, or demon race, was transformed into the animals and other objects whose names they bore and still bear. The souls of the present race are not supposed to undergo transmigration.—G. G.

wolves said, "Kwahtie, you tell lies, for I can smell something, and my nose tells me that you have killed our chief." "Well," says Kwahtie, "if you think so, call all your tribe here, and I will work spells, and you can then see whether I have killed him or not." Accordingly they all came. Kwahtie told them to form a circle, leaving an opening on one side, which they did. He then took a bottle or bladder of oil in one hand, and a comb with very long teeth in the other, and commenced a song in which he at first denied all knowledge of the chief, but at length admitted the fact, upon which he started and ran out of the circle, dashing down the bladder of oil which turned into water. He also stuck his comb into the sand, which was immediately changed into the rocks from Clyoquot to Flattery rocks. He then dived into the water and escaped. It was in this manner, said my informant, that Neeah Bay and the Straits were formed; for the land formerly was level and good, till Kwahtie turned it into rocks and water. Kwahtie was a great magician till the Ho-hó-c-ap-béss transformed him. He had the choice offered him of being a bird or a fish, but declined both. He was then told that as he was fond of fish he might live on land and eat what fish he could catch or pick up.

The raven, Klook-shood, was a strong Indian very fond of flesh, a sort of cannibal, as was his wife Cha-ká-do, the crow, and their strong beaks were given them to tear their food, whether fish, flesh, or vegetable, for they had great appetites, and devoured everything they could find. The crane, Kwáh-less, was a great fisherman, always on the rocks, or wading about, with his long fish spear ready to transfix his prey. He constantly wore the tsá-sa-ka-dup, or little circular cape, worn by the Makahs during wet weather while fishing. This was turned into the feathers about his neck, and his fish spear into his long bill. The kingfisher, Chesh-kully, was also a fisherman, but a thief, and had stolen a necklace of the Che-tóh-dook or dentalium shells; these were turned into the ring of white feathers about his neck.

At the time of the transformation of Indians into animals, there was no wood in the land, nothing but grass and sand, so the Ho-hó-c-ap-béss, mindful of the wants of the future inhabitants, prepared for them fuel. To one they said, you are old, and your heart is dry, you will make good kindling wood, for your grease has turned hard and will make pitch (kluk-ait-a-biss), your name is Do-hó-bupt, and you shall be the spruce tree, which when it grows old will always make dry wood. To another, your name is Kla-ká-bupt, and you shall be the hemlock. The Indians will want some harder wood, and therefore Kwahk-sá-bupt, you shall be the alder, and you, Dopt-kó-bupt, shall be the crab apple, and as you have a cross temper you shall bear sour fruit. The Indians will likewise want tough wood to make bows, and wedges with which to split logs; you Kla-haik'-tle-bup are tough and strong, and therefore you shall be the yew tree. They will also require soft lasting wood to make canoes, you Kla-áe-sook shall be the cedar. And thus they give the origin of every tree, shrub, or herb.

The cause of the ebb and flow of the tides is accounted for in this manner. The raven, Klook-shood, not being contented with his one wife, the crow, went up the straits and stole the daughter of Tu-chee, the east wind. Tu-chee, after searching twenty days, found him, and a compromise was effected, by which the raven was to receive some land as a present. At that time the tide did not ebb and flow, so Tu-chee promised he would make the waters retire for twenty days, and during that time Klook-shood might pick up what he could find on the flats to eat. Klook-shood was not satisfied with this, but wanted the land to be made bare as far as the cape. Tu-chee said no, he would only make it dry for a few feet. Klook-shood told him he was a very mean fellow, and that he had better take his daughter back again. At last the matter was settled by Tu-chee agreeing to make the water leave the flats twice every twenty-four hours. This was deemed satisfactory, and thus it was that the ebb and flow of the tide was caused, to enable the ravens and crows to go on the flats and pick up the food left by the water.

The Dukwally and other tamánawas performances are exhibitions intended to represent incidents connected with their mythological legends. There are a great variety, and they seem to take the place, in a measure, of theatrical performances or games during the season of the religious festivals. There are no persons especially set apart as priests for the performance of these ceremonies, although some, who seem more expert than others, are usually hired to give life to the scenes, but these performers are quite as often found among the slaves or common people as among the chiefs, and excepting during the continuance of the festivities are not looked on as of any particular importance. On inquiring the origin of these ceremonies, I was informed that they did not originate with the Indians, but were revelations of the guardian spirits, who made known what they wished to be performed. An Indian, for instance, who has been consulting with his guardian spirit, which is done by going through the washing and fasting process before described, will imagine or think he is called upon to represent the owl; he arranges in his mind the style of dress, the number of performers, the songs and dances or other movements, and having the plan perfected, announces at a tamánawas meeting that he has had a revelation which he will impart to a select few. These are then taught and drilled in strict secrecy, and when they have perfected themselves, will suddenly make their appearance and perform before the astonished tribe. Another Indian gets up the representation of the whale, others do the same of birds, and in fact of everything that they can think of. If any performance is a success, it is repeated, and gradually comes to be looked upon as one of the regular order in the ceremonies; if it does not satisfy the audience, it is laid aside. Thus they have performances that have been handed down from remote ages, while others are of a more recent date. My residence in the school building, but a stone's throw from the houses at Neeah village, gave me an excellent opportunity to see all the performances that the uninitiated are permitted to witness, and to hear all the din of their out-door and in-door operations.

The ceremony of the great Dukwally, or the Thunder bird, originated with the Hesh-kwi-et Indians, a band of Nittinats living near Barclay Sound, Vancouver Island, and is ascribed to the following legend:—

Two men had fallen in love with one woman, and as she would give neither the preference, at last they came to a quarrel. But one of them, who had better sense than the other, said, Don't let us fight about that squaw; I will go out and see the chief of the wolves, and he will tell me what is to be done; but I cannot get to his lodge except by stratagem. Now they know we are at variance, so do you take me by the hair, and drag me over these sharp rocks which are covered with barnacles, and I shall bleed, and I will pretend to be dead, and the wolves will come and carry me away to their house. The other agreed, and dragged him over the rocks till he was lacerated from head to foot, and then left him out of reach of the tide. The wolves came, and supposing him dead, carried him to the lodge of their chief; but when they got ready to eat him, he jumped up and astonished them at his boldness. The chief wolf was so much pleased with his bravery, that he imparted to him all the mysteries of the Thunder bird performance, and on his return home he instructed his friends, and the Dukwally was the result. The laceration of the arms and legs among the Makahs, during the performance to be described, is to represent the laceration of the founder of the ceremony from being dragged over the sharp stones.

A person intending to give one of these performances first gathers together as much property as he can obtain, in blankets, guns, brass kettles, beads, tin pans, and other articles intended as presents for his guests, and procures a sufficient quantity of food, which of late years consists of flour, biscuit, rice, potatoes, molasses, dried fish, and roots. He keeps his intention a secret until he is nearly ready, and then imparts it to a few of his friends, who if need be assist him by adding to his stock of presents or food. The first intimation the village has of the intended ceremonies is on the night previous to the first day's performance. After the community have retired for the night, which is usually between nine and ten o'clock, the performers commence by hooting like owls, howling like wolves, and uttering a sharp whistling sound intended to represent the blowing and whistling of the wind. Guns are then fired, and all the initiated collect in the lodge where the ceremonies are to be performed, and drum with their heels on boxes or boards, producing a sound resembling thunder. The torches of pitch wood are flashed through the roof of the house, and at each flash the thunder rolls, and then the whole assemblage whistles like the wind. As soon as the noise of the performers commences, the uninitiated fly in terror and hide themselves, so great being their superstitious belief in the supernatural powers of the Dukwally, that they have frequently fled to my house for protection, knowing very well that the tamánawas performers would not come near a white man. They then visit every house in the village, and extend an invitation for all to attend the ceremonies. This having been done, the crowd retire to the lodge of ceremonies, where the drumming and singing are kept up till near daylight, when they are quiet for a short time, and at sunrise begin again. The first five days are usually devoted to secret ceremonies, such as initiating candidates, and a variety of performances which consist chiefly in songs and chorus and drumming to imitate thunder. They do this part very well, and their imitation of thunder is quite equal to that produced in the best equipped theatre.

What the ceremony of initiation is I have never learned. That of the Clallams, which I have witnessed, consists in putting the initiates into a mesmeric sleep; but if the Makahs use mesmerism, or any such influence, they do not keep the candidates under it for any great length of time, as I saw them every day during the ceremonies, walking out during the intervals. The first out-door performance usually commences on the fifth day, and this consists of the procession of males and females, with their legs and arms, and sometimes their bodies, scarified with knives, and every wound bleeding freely. The men are entirely naked, but the women have on a short petticoat. I had seen this performance several times, and had always been told by the Indians that the cutting was done by the principal performers, or medicine men, who seized all they could get hold of, and thus lacerated them; but I have since been admitted to a lodge to witness the operation. I expected the performers would be in a half frantic state, cutting and slashing regardless of whom they might wound; I, however, found it otherwise. A bucket of water was placed in the centre of the lodge, and the candidates squatting around it washed their arms and legs. The persons who did the cutting, and who appeared to be any one who had sharp knives, butcher-knives being preferred, grasped them firmly in the right hand with the thumb placed along the blade, so as to leave but an eighth or quarter of an inch of the edge bare; then, taking hold of the arm or leg of the candidate, made gashes five or six inches long transversely, and parallel with the limb, four or five gashes being cut each way. Cuts were thus made on each arm above and below the elbow, on each thigh, and the calves of the legs; some, but not all, were likewise cut on their backs. The wounds were then washed with water to make the blood run freely. The persons operated on did not seem to mind it all, but laughed and chatted with each other until all were ready to go out, and then they set up a dismal howling; but I think the pain they felt could not be very great, for two Indians who went in with me, seeing there were but few in the procession, asked me if I would like to see them join in. I told them I should like very well to see the performance; upon which they deliberately pulled off their blankets and shirts, and continued in conversation with me while their arms and legs were gashed in the same manner. An Indian must be possessed of a much lower degree of nervous organization than a white man to suffer such operations and show no more feeling. Some may think it stoical indifference, but certainly such a scoring of the body would throw a white man into a fever. The same two Indians came to me about an hour after the performance had closed, and although their wounds had bled freely, they assured me they felt no pain. Sometimes, however, the cuts are accidentally made deep, and produce sores. When all was ready the procession left the lodge, and marched in single file down to the beach; their naked bodies streaming with blood presenting a barbarous spectacle. A circle was formed at the water's edge, round which this bloody procession marched slowly, making gesticulations and uttering howling cries.

Five men now came out of the lodge carrying the principal performer. One held him by the hair, and the others by the arms and legs. He too was cut and bleeding profusely. They laid him down on the beach on the wet sand, and left him, while they marched off and visited every lodge in the village, making a circuit in each lodge. At last the man on the beach jumped up, and seizing a club laid about him in a violent manner, hitting everything in his way. He too went the same round as the others, and after every lodge had been visited they all returned to the lodge from which they had issued, and the performances, out-

THE INDIANS OF CAPE FLATTERY. 69

door, were closed for that day. In the meanwhile a deputation of fifteen or twenty men, with faces painted black and sprigs of evergreen in their hair, had been sent to the other villages with invitations for guests to come and receive presents. They went in a body to each lodge, and after a song and a chorus, the spokesman of the party in a loud voice announced the object of their visit, and called the names of the invited persons. Any one has a right to be present at the distribution, but only those specially invited will receive any presents.

Every evening during the ceremonies, excepting those of the first few days, is devoted to masquerade and other amusements, when each lodge is visited and a performance enacted. Some of the masks are frightful objects, as may be seen in Figures 35—41. They are made principally by the Clyoquot and Nittinat Indians,

Fig. 35. No. 2714. Fig. 36. No. 4119.

Fig. 37. Fig 38

and sold to the Makahs, who paint them to suit their own fancies. They are made of alder, maple, and cottonwood; some are very ingeniously executed, having the eyes and lower jaw movable. By means of a string the performer can make the eyes roll about, and the jaws gnash together with a fearful clatter. As these masks are kept strictly concealed until the time of the performances, and as

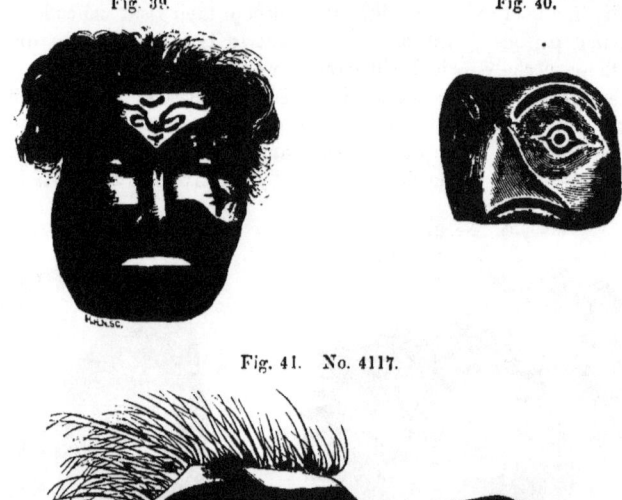

Fig. 39.　　　　　Fig. 40.

Fig. 41.　No. 4117.

they are generally produced at night, they are viewed with awe by the spectators; and certainly the scene in one of these lodges, dimly lighted by the fires which show the faces of the assembled spectators and illuminate the performers, presents a most weird and savage spectacle when the masked dancers issue forth from behind a screen of mats, and go through their barbarous pantomimes. The Indians themselves, even accustomed as they are to these masks, feel very much afraid of them, and a white man, viewing the scene for the first time, can only liken it to a carnival of demons.

Among the masquerade performances that I have seen was a representation of mice. This was performed by a dozen or more young men who were entirely naked. Their bodies, limbs, and faces were painted with stripes of red, blue, and black; red bark wreaths were twisted around their heads, and bows and arrows in their hands. They made a squealing noise, but otherwise they did nothing that reminded me of mice in the least. Another party was composed of naked boys, with bark fringes, like veils, covering their faces, and armed with sticks having needles in one end; they made a buzzing noise, and stuck the needles into any of the spectators who came in their way. This was a representation of hornets. These processions followed each other at an interval of half an hour, and each made a circuit round the lodge, performed some antics, sang some songs, shouted, and left. Another party then came in, composed of men with frightful masks, bear-skins on their backs, and heads covered with down. They had clubs in their hands, and as they danced around a big fire blazing in the centre of the lodge, they struck wildly with them, caring little whom or what they hit. One of their number was naked, with a rope round his waist, a knife in each hand, and making a fearful howling. Two others had hold of the end of the rope as if to keep him from doing any harm. This was the most ferocious exhibition I had seen, and the spectators got out of their reach as far as they could. They did no harm, however, excepting that one with his club knocked a hole through a brass kettle; after which they left and went to the other lodges, when I learned that they smashed boxes and did much mischief. After they had gone the owner examined his kettle, and quaintly remarked that it was worth more to him than the pleasure he had experienced by their visit, and he should look to the man who broke it for remuneration.

On a subsequent evening I was present at another performance. This consisted of dancing, jumping, firing of guns, etc. A large fire was first built in the centre of the lodge, and the performers, with painted faces, and many with masks resembling owls, wolves, and bears, crouched down with their arms clasped about their knees, their blankets trailing on the ground, and fastened around the neck with a single pin. After forming in a circle with their faces towards the fire, they commenced jumping sideways round the blaze, their arms still about their knees. In this manner they whirled around for several minutes, producing a most remarkable appearance. These performers, who were male, were succeeded by some thirty women* with blackened faces, their heads covered with down, and a girdle around their blankets drawing them in tight at the waist. These danced around the fire with a shuffling, ungainly gait, singing a song as loud as they could scream, which was accompanied by every one in the lodge, and beating time with sticks on boards placed before them for the purpose. When the dance was over, some five or six men, with wreaths of sea-weed around their heads, blackened faces, and bear-skins over their shoulders, rushed in and fired a volley of musketry through the roof. One of them then made a speech, the purport of which was that the ceremonies had progressed favorably thus far, that their hearts had become strong, and that they felt ready to attack their enemies, or to repel any attack upon themselves. Their guns having in the meanwhile been loaded, another volley was fired and the whole assembly uttered a shout to signify approval. The performances during the daytime consisted of representations on the beach of various kinds. There was one representing a whaling scene. An Indian on all fours, covered with a bear-skin, imitated the motion of a whale while blowing. He was followed by a party of eight men armed with harpoons and lances, and carrying all the implements of whaling. Two boys, naked, with bodies rubbed over with flour, and white cloths around their heads, represented cold weather; others represented cranes, moving slowly at the water's edge, and occasionally dipping their heads down as if seizing a fish. They wore masks resembling a bird's beak, and bunches of eagle's feathers stuck in their hair. During all of these scenes the spectators kept up a continual singing and drumming. Every day during these performances feasts were given at different lodges to those Indians who had come from the other villages, at which great quantities of food were eaten and many cords of wood burned, the giver of the feast being very prodigal of his winter's supply of food and fuel. The latter, however, is procured quite easily from the forest, and only causes a little extra labor to obtain a sufficiency.

The final exhibition of the ceremonies was the T'hlūkloots representation, after which the presents were distributed. From daylight in the morning till about eleven o'clock in the forenoon was occupied by indoor performances, consisting of singing and drumming, and occasional speeches. When these were over, some twenty performers dressed up in masks and feathers, some with naked bodies, others covered with bear skins, and accompanied by the whole assembly, went down on the beach and danced and howled in the most frightful manner. After making as much uproar as they could, they returned to the lodge, and shortly after every one mounted on the roofs of the houses to see the performance of the T'hlūkloots. First, a young girl came out upon the roof of a lodge wearing a mask representing the head of the thunder bird, which was surmounted by a top-knot of cedar bark dyed red and stuck full of white feathers from eagles' tails. Over her shoulders she wore a red blanket covered with a profusion of white buttons, brass thimbles and blue beads; her hair hung down her back covered with white down. The upper half of her face was painted black and the lower red. Another girl with a similar headdress, was naked except a skirt about her hips. Her arms and legs had rings of blue beads, and she wore bracelets of brass wire around her wrists; her face being painted like the other. A smaller girl had a black mask to resemble the ha-hék-to-ak. The masks did not cover the face, but were on the forehead, from which they projected like horns. The last girl's face was also painted black and red. From her ears hung large ornaments made of the haikwa or dentalium, and blue and red beads, and around her neck was an immense necklace of blue beads. Her skirt was also covered with strings of beads, giving her quite a picturesque appearance. A little boy with a black mask and head-band of red bark, the ends of which hung down over his shoulders, and eagles' feathers in a top-knot, was the remaining performer. They moved around in a slow and stately manner, occasionally spreading out their arms to represent flying and uttering a sound to imitate thunder, but which resembled the noise made by the nighthawk when swooping for its prey, the spectators meanwhile beating drums, pounding the roofs with sticks, and rattling with shells. This show lasted half an hour, when all again went into the lodge to witness the distribution of presents and the grand finale. The company all being arranged, the performers at one end of the lodge and the women, children, and spectators at the other, they commenced by putting out the fires and removing the brands and cinders. A quantity of feathers were strewed over the ground floor of the lodge, and a dance and song commenced, every one joining in the latter, each seeming to try to make as much noise as possible. A large box, suspended by a rope from the roof, served as a bass drum, and other drums were improvised from the brass and sheet-iron kettles and tin pans belonging to the domestic furniture of the house, while those who had no kettles, pans, or boxes, banged with their clubs on the roof and sides of the house till the noise was almost deafening. In this uproar there was a pause, then the din commenced anew. This time the dancers brought out blankets, and with them beat the feathers on the floor till the whole air was filled with down, like flakes of snow during a heavy winter's storm. Another lull succeeded, then another dance, and another shaking up of feathers, till I was half choked with dust and down. Next the presents were distributed, consisting of blankets, guns, shirts, beads, and a variety of trinkets, and the whole affair wound up with a feast.

This was the Dukwally or "black tamánawas" ceremony. It is exhibited every winter, sometimes at only one village and sometimes at all.

The other performance is termed Tsiahk, and is a medicine performance, quite as interesting, but not as savage in its detail. It is only occasionally performed, when some person, either a chief or a member of his family, is sick. The Makahs believe in the existence of a supernatural being, who is represented to be an Indian of a dwarfish size, with long hair of a yellowish color flowing down his back and covering his shoulders. From his head grow four perpendicular horns, two at the temple and two back of the ears. When people are sick of any chronic complaint and much debilitated, they imagine they see this being in the night, who promises relief if the ceremonies he prescribes are well performed. The principal performer is a doctor, whose duties are to manipulate the patient, who is first initiated by secret rites into the mysteries of the ceremony. What these secret rites consist of I have not ascertained, but there is a continual singing and drumming during the day and evening for three days before spectators are admitted. From the haggard and feeble appearance of some patients I have seen, I judge the ordeal must have been severe. The peculiarity of this ceremony consists in the dress worn alike by patients, novitiates, and performers. Both men and women assist, but the proportion of females is greater than of males. Fig. 42 shows a back view of a female performer in full dress; on her head is worn a sort of coronet made of bark, surmounted by four upright bunches or little pillars, made of bark wound round with the same material, and, sometimes threads from red blankets to give a variety of color. From the top of each of the four pillars, which represent the horns of the tsiahk, are bunches of eagles' quills, which have been notched, and one side of the feather edge stripped off. In front is a band, which is variously decorated, according to the taste of the wearer, with beads, brass buttons, or any trinkets they may have. From each side of this band project bunches of quills similar to those on the top of the head. The long hair of the Tsiahk is represented by a heavy and thick fringe of bark, which covers the back and shoulders to the elbow. Necklaces composed of a great many strings of beads of all sizes and colors, and strung in various forms, are also worn, and serve to add to the effect of the costume. The paint for the face is red for the forehead and for the lower part, from the root of the nose to the ears; the portion between the forehead and the lower part is black with two or three red marks on each cheek. The dress of the novitiate females is similar, with the exception of there being no feathers or ornaments on the bark

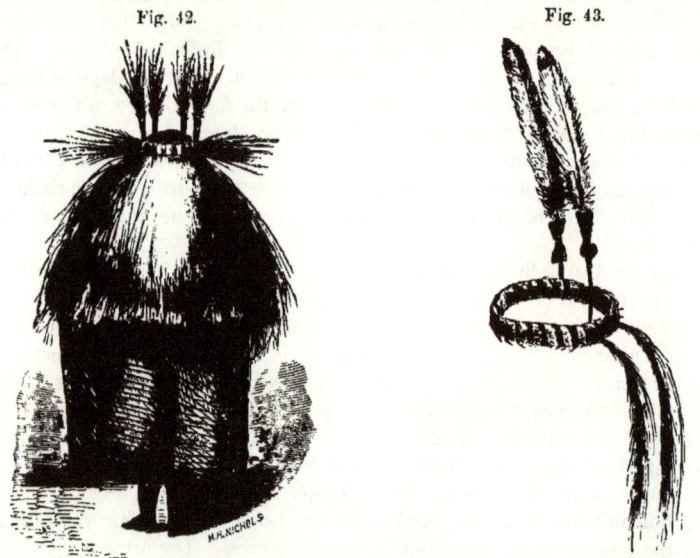

Fig. 42.   Fig. 43.

headdress, and with the addition of black or blue stripes on the red paint covering the forehead and lower portion of the face. The headdress of the men (Fig. 43) consists of a circular band of bark and colored worsted, from the back part of which are two bunches of bark, like horses' tails. Two upright sticks are fastened to the band behind the ears, and on top of these sticks are two white feathers tipped with red; the quill portion is inserted into a piece of elder stick with the pith extracted, and then put on the band sticks. These sockets give the feathers the charm of vibrating as the wearer moves his head; when dancing or moving in procession the hands are raised as high as the face, and the fingers spread out.

The doctor or principal performer has on his head a dress of plain bark similar to the female novitiate. He is naked except a piece of blanket about his loins, and his body is covered with stripes of red paint. The out-door performance consists of a procession which moves from the lodge to the beach; the principal actor or conductor being at the head, followed by all the males in single file, the last one being the doctor. Immediately behind the doctor the patient follows, supported on each side by a female assistant. The females close up the procession. All parties, male and female, have their hands raised as high as their faces, and the motion of the procession is a sort of shuffling dance. They move in a circle which gradually closes around the patient, who, with the novitiate, is left seated on the ground in the centre; songs with choruses by the whole of the spectators, drumming, shaking rattles, and firing of guns wind up the performance, and all retire to the lodge, where dancing and singing are kept up for several days. Finally, presents are distributed, a feast is held, and the friends retire. The patient and novitiates are obliged to wear their dress for one month. It consists of the bark headdress, having, instead of feathers, two thin strips of wood, feather-shaped, but differently painted. Those of the patient are red at each end and white in the centre, with narrow transverse bars of blue. Those of the novitiate have blue ends and the centre unpainted. The patient's face is painted red, with perpendicular marks of blue on the forehead and the lower part of the face. The noviciate's forehead and lower portion of face is painted with alternate stripes of red and blue, the remainder of the face blue; the head band is also wound with blue yarn and yellow bark. The head-band of the patient is wound with red. The tails of bark of both headdresses are dyed red. The patient carries in his hand a staff which can be used as a support while walking; this has red bark tied at each end and around the middle.

The Dukwally and Tsiahk are the performances more frequently exhibited among the Makahs than any others, although they have several different ones. The ancient tamánawas is termed Do-t'hlub or Do-t'hlnm, and was formerly the favorite one. But after they had learned the T'hūlkloots or Thunder Bird, they laid aside the Do-t'hlub, as its performance, from the great number of ceremonies, was attended with too much trouble and expense. The origin of the Do-t'hlub was, as stated to me by the Indians, in this manner: many years ago, an Indian while fishing in deep water for codfish, hauled up on his hook an immense haliotis shell. He had scarcely got it into his canoe when he fell into a trance which lasted a few minutes, and on his recovery he commenced paddling home, but before reaching land he had several of these trances, and on reaching the shore his friends took him up for dead, and carried him into his house, where he presently recovered, and stated, that while in the state of stupor he had a vision of Do-t'hlub, one of their mythological beings, and that he must be dressed as Do-t'hlub was and then he would have revelations. He described the appearance, as he saw it in his vision, in which Do-t'hlub presented himself with hands like deer's feet. He was naked to his hips, around which was a petticoat of cedar bark dyed red, which reached to his knees. His body and arms were red; his face painted red and black; his hair tied up in bunches with cedar twigs, and cedar twigs reaching down his back. When his friends had dressed him according to his direction, he fell into another trance, in which he saw the dances which were to be performed, heard the songs which were to be sung, and learned all the secret ceremonies to be observed. It was also revealed that each performer must have a piece of the haliotis shell in his nose, and pieces in his ears. He taught the rites to certain of his friends, and then performed before the tribe, who were so well pleased that they adopted the ceremony as their tamánawas, and retained its observance for many years, till it was superseded by the Dukwally. The haliotis shell worn by the Makahs in their noses is a custom originating from the Do-t'hlub. Other ceremonies are occasionally gone through with, but the description above given will serve to illustrate all those observed by the Makahs. Different tribes have some peculiar to themselves, the general character of which is, however, the same. It will be seen that the public part of these performances are rather in the nature of amusements akin to our theatrical pantomimes than of religious observances, though they are religiously observed.

The Makahs, like all other Indians, are exceedingly superstitious, believing in dreams, in revelations, necromancy, and in the power of individuals over the elements. An instance of the latter fell under my own observation. Early in April, 1864, there was a continuance of stormy weather which prevented them from going after whales or fishing. At length an Indian, who came from the Hosett village at Flattery Rocks informed me that his people had found out that Keyattic, an old man living with them, had caused the bad weather. A woman and a boy had found him at his incantations and reported him to the tribe; whereupon the whole village went to Keyattic's lodge, and told him that if he did not immediately stop and make fair weather, they would hang him. He promised to do so, and they gave him two days to calm the wind and sea. The Indian added with great gravity that now we should have fair weather. I told him that it was foolish talk. He said no, that the Indians in former times were capable of making it rain or blow at pleasure, and cited a recent case of a Kwilléyute Indian, who only a few summers previous had made bad weather during the halibut season. The Kwilléyutes hung him, and immediately the weather became fair. In the present instance we did have fair weather in two days after, and the Indians were confirmed in the belief that old Keyattic had caused the storm that prevented their going out in canoes, and that the fear of death had forced him to allay it. Through dreams they think they can foretell events and predict the sickness or death of their friends. Some are supposed to be more gifted in this respect than others, and many a marvellous tale has been related to me by these dreamers; but in every instance the events had already taken place which they pretended to have predicted. Their necromancy consists in the performance of the doctors, which will be alluded to more at length under the heading of "medicine."

It will be seen that though the Makahs are heathens in the fullest sense, they are not idolaters or worshippers of images, but that their secret addresses are to the sun as the representative of the Great Spirit. They seem, on the other hand, perfectly indifferent to teaching. They will not believe that the white man's God is the same as their Great Chief, nor give any attention to the truths of Christianity. If the children could be removed from their parents and the influences of the tribe, and placed in a civilized community, they might be led to embrace our religion as well as customs; but any efforts of a missionary on the spot, opposed as they would be by prejudice, superstition, and indifference, would be futile. The most that can be hoped for, at present, is to keep them at peace, and gradually teach them such simple matters as they can be made to take an interest in, and will tend to ameliorate their condition.

MAGIC AND "MEDICINE."—The Makahs have, as usual, certain persons, both male and female, who are supposed to be skilled in the art of healing. The male practitioners alone, however, go through an ordeal or tamánawas to constitute them "doctors." An ancient ceremony called Ka-háip was formerly always observed to endow them with supernatural powers, but it is seldom used of late years, and there are but three persons living in the tribe at present who have undertaken it. They obtain notoriety by occasional good fortune in apparently performing remarkable

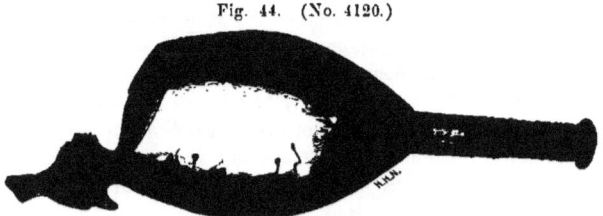

Fig. 44. (No. 4120.)

Rattle used by medicine men.

cures, and each is celebrated for some faculty peculiar to himself in removing disease. Every sickness for which they cannot assign some obvious cause is supposed to be the work of a "skoo-koom," or demon, who enters the mouth when drinking at a brook, or pierces the skin while bathing in salt water. These evil spirits assume the form of a little white worm which the doctor extracts by means of manipulations, and the patient recovers. Although I have repeatedly seen them at work on their patients, and pretending to take out these animals, I have never seen the object itself, which, as they generally informed me, is only seen by the doctor. In extracting these pretended evil spirits, he manipulates the part affected, frequently washing the hands during the operation, and warming them at the fire. This, he states, is to make the hands sensitive, so that on pressing them upon the patient's body he can the more easily feel where the evil is located. Sometimes he is an hour or two in finding the skoo-koom, particularly if the patient be a chief, as then not only the doctor's fees will be larger, but there will probably be a great company of friends assembled to sing and drum, and afterwards to feast.

When the doctor thinks that he has worked enough, he will then try to catch the *skookoom* and squeeze it out. If he succeeds, he blows through his hand toward the roof of the lodge, and assures the patient that it has gone. An instance occurred about Christmas time, 1864, of an old man who had been sick for two or three years of lingering consumption. He had exerted himself very much at a Dukwally performance, and by some violent strain had burst an abscess on his lungs and was in a very critical condition. I was sent for, and told he was dying, and went immediately to his lodge, where I found him under the immediate charge of an Indian doctor. By virtue of my position as dispenser of medicines for the reservation, I was permitted to remain as a sort of consulting physician. I was perfectly well aware of the circumstances attending the case, and that the patient was dying, and simply took with me an anodyne to relieve the pain of his last moments; but as I could do nothing while the Indian doctor was at work, I remained a spectator of the scene. The patient was upon his knees, his head supported by an Indian who was in front of him. The doctor, a muscular, powerful man, having washed his hands and warmed them, grasped the patient by the back of the neck, pressing his thumbs against the spinal column, and moving them with all his might as though he was trying to separate the skull from the backbone. He exerted himself to such a degree that every muscle and vein was distended, and drops of perspiration ran freely from his face. At length he gave a wrench and a twist, the patient uttered a yell, when it was announced to me by the doctor that the *skookoom* had been caught, and that the man would recover. I told him the man would die in half an hour, but if he had not been squeezed so hard, and had taken my medicine, he would possibly have lived two or three days. The doctor laughed, and replied that I did not know as well as the Indians did; but it proved as I predicted. The man did die, and in less than two hours from the time I had made the remark he was buried, myself assisting in the ceremonies, as I desired to see how they were performed.

They have a variety of songs and chants during the performance, each doctor seeming to have a tune of his own. But the method adopted by all, is first to remove the *skookoom* by manipulation, and after that administer other remedies. Some of the old women are skilled as physicians both in the above method and in the preparation of medicinal herbs. I saw the application of a most singular remedy in the case of a young man who had been shot through the left arm by a dragoon pistol, in the hand of another Indian who was drunk. The ball passed through the arm between the shoulder and the elbow, injuring, but not breaking the bone, and lodged in the muscles of the back, from whence it was extracted in a rude manner by an incision made with a jack-knife. I advised the friends to take him immediately to Port Angeles or Victoria, where he could have surgical advice, but they concluded to try their own remedies first. They attempted to stop the bleeding by applying hemlock bark chewed fine, which seemed to have the desired effect. They next went to where the young man's father was buried, and dug up the bone of the upper part of the left arm, which they washed, and then sawed or split in two, lengthwise, and formed splints of it. These were scraped, and the scrapings of the bone applied as a dressing. The bone splints were applied and the arm bandaged firmly. The Indians assured me that the bone from the father's arm would renew or replace the wounded one in the boy's arm; that they always tried it in the case of a broken bone, and it always effected a cure. Thus, if a leg, an arm, or a rib is broken, they take a similar one from the body of the nearest relative who has been dead over a year, and apply it either as a dressing by scraping, or in the form of splints. I have, however, seen none but the instance above quoted where the splints were applied. In this case fragments of the bone continually coming away, the remedy proved worthless, and after several months' suffering, the young man was carried to Victoria, where the arm was attended to by a skilful surgeon, and he shortly recovered. There is not an instance in the whole tribe where an amputation has been performed, although I have known several cases where life would have been saved had the patient or his friends submitted to or allowed the operation. But as they know nothing of the practice themselves, they are very reluctant to have any such operations performed, preferring death to the loss of a limb. Incised wounds and lacerations are treated either with a poultice of chewed hemlock, or elder bark, or wood ashes strewed on, which absorbs the discharge and forms a crust or scab. Wounds of this description heal very readily, which is to be wondered at, since their systems are so full of humors, but it is very rare that suppuration occurs; although in several instances of bruises on the leg, or the skin, I have seen bad ulcers that were a long time healing.

The whole tribe are pervaded by a scrofulous or strumous diathesis which shows itself in all its various forms; enlargement and suppuration of the cervical glands; strumous ulcers in the armpits, and swelling and suppuration in the groin and thigh. The strumous bubo is of common occurrence in infants, children of all ages, and adults. These are invariably cut, I cannot say lanced, for the instrument in all cases is a knife, and the wounds allowed to take care of themselves. Sores of this description are considered by most of the white people of the territory to be of syphilitic origin, but I am of opinion that such is not the case. This tribe is remarkably exempt from diseases of a venereal nature; and in a residence of three years among them, during two of which I have dispensed medicines, but three cases have come to my observation of syphilitic bubo. One was a squaw, who had contracted the disease in Victoria; the other two, men of the tribe to whom on her return she had imparted it; but I think I can safely assert that there is scarcely an individual in the whole tribe but what has had strumous buboes or ulcerations of the cervical glands at some period of life. Eruptive diseases, such as scald head, ringworm, and a species of itch, are very common among infants; all of which, and their scrofulous tumors, may be attributed to filthy habits and the nature of their food, which consists chiefly of fish and oil. A variety of the thorn oyster is frequently thrown ashore after heavy storms; or is found in the root of the kelp which has grown upon it, and, being torn up by the breakers, brings the oyster ashore in its grasp. These are not eaten, but I have seen the fresh ones made use of as a sort of poultice for boils, and also raw fish is occasionally applied to the same purpose. Sometimes, when they wish to apply a rubefacient to tumors, they use *Pyrola elliptica*, which is bruised into a pulpy mass, and applied by means of a bandage. This little plant is very common in the woods, and is capable of producing a blister on the skin of a white person; but the Indians seldom retain it long enough to create anything more than a redness or inflammation of the part.

One of their remedies to reduce a strumous tumor is by means of actual cautery, prepared from the dried inner bark of the white pine, which is applied by a moxa or cone. The skin is first wet with saliva at the desired point; the moxa then placed upon it and set on fire. The bark burns very rapidly and causes a deep sore, which is kept open by removing the scab as often as it forms, until relief is felt. Sometimes they apply several of these moxas to the person at one time. I have seen them give relief in many instances. This practice seems to be a common one among all the coast tribes in the vicinity, and it is rare to see an adult who has not scars produced by its means.

Burning the flesh is also resorted to for other purposes. Boys will apply moxas made of dried and partially charred pitch, to the back of the thumbs from the nail to the wrist. When the sores heal, they leave scars or callous spots, which are supposed not only to keep the bow-strings from hurting the hand, but to give a steadiness of aim, so that they can throw their arrows with more precision. I have seen school-boys sit down of an evening by the fire and amuse themselves in this manner, holding out their hands with the burning pitch singing into the flesh, and showing their bravery by the amount of pain they could bear. I usually found, however, that they were very willing for me to dress their hands with salve whenever they had attempted this performance. Blood-letting is not practised according to our methods, but in case of bruises when there is swelling and much pain, they scarify the skin by cutting longitudinal and transverse gashes just deep enough to make the blood flow by keeping the part moistened with water. Cauterizing the flesh is, however, the favorite and most generally practised remedy for all internal complaints, and answers with the Indian the double purpose of blisters and bleeding.

There are many cases of deformity arising from strumous disease of hip-joint, white swelling of the knee, and rheumatic affection of feet. These cripples go about with the aid of a stick or pole, which they hold with both hands. I have made crutches for some, but they could never be persuaded to use them. There is one case of enlargement of the scrotum to an enormous size. The patient is a man about forty years of age, who has been troubled with the complaint for about twenty years, the sac gradually enlarging, so that now it reaches four inches below the knee and is of the size of a five gallon keg. He assures me that he suffers no pain from it, but the enormous size is quite inconvenient, and causes him to walk with a very peculiar gait. As his only covering is a blanket, the parts are frequently exposed. The complaint does not appear to be dropsical, but rather an adipose secretion. Doctor Davies, formerly physician and surgeon to the reservation, was desirous of making an examination, but the man was exceedingly opposed to it, and no opportunity has been had of ascertaining its real character.

The most common complaints are diarrhœa and dysentery, coughs, colds, and consumption. The first two are most frequent, and have been formerly very fatal. I find, however, that taken in their early stages they readily yield to simple treatment, and a dose of castor oil, followed by Dover's powder from five to ten grains, is quite sufficient in most cases to effect a cure. During my experience among the coast Indians for a period of more than twelve years, I have noticed, as a general rule, that they require less medicine than white men, and invariably when administering any (with the exception of castor oil), I have given but one-half the amount that would be given to one of the latter. There seem to be no general remedies among themselves, each doctor or doctress having his or her own peculiar herbs, roots, or bark which they prepare in secret and administer with ceremony. I have seen a woman pulverize charcoal and mix it with water for her child to drink, who had a diarrhœa. Some make a tea of hemlock bark for an astringent, others scrape that of the wild currant, elder, or wild cherry, and make tea of it.

The *Polypodium falcatum?* or, as it is commonly called, the sweet liquorice fern, is a most excellent alterative, and is much used by both white persons and Indians in the territory, having acquired a reputation in venereal complaints. In the form of a decoction it is an excellent medicine combined with iodide of potassium. There are two varieties found at Cape Flattery; one growing on the trunks of trees or old mossy logs; the other on the rocks. The plants are similar in general appearance, except that those growing on rocks have a stout, fleshy leaf. The taste of the roots and their medicinal virtues appear to be the same. From the very many evidences I have had of their beneficial effects, I am led to conclude that their virtues far surpass those of the *P. vulgare*, which was formerly of great repute, but which has been laid aside in modern practice. Perhaps the *Polypodium* growing upon the immediate sea-coast derives some peculiar quality from the atmosphere of the ocean, but it certainly seems to be as efficacious and to take the place in this latitude of the sarsaparilla of the equatorial regions. By the white settlers it is often mixed with the root of the "Oregon grape" (*Mahonia*), but the Makahs use it alone, either simply chewing it and swallowing the juice, or boiling it with water and drinking the decoction. A number of species of liverwort are found at Cape Flattery, one of which grows upon the ground, and when freshly gathered has the taste of spruce leaves. The Indians use this for coughs, and as a diuretic. When chewed it appears to be of a mucilaginous nature, somewhat like slippery elm. It loses its peculiar spruce flavor on being dried, and I think its virtues are greatest when the plant is green. A variety of bittersweet or wintergreen is used for derangement of the stomach and intestinal canal. This is simply chewed and swallowed. I was shown one day by a sick chief, a great medicine which he had received from a Clyoquot doctor. It was kept very secret, and I was permitted to examine it as a mark of great confidence and friendship. After a number of rags had been unrolled, a little calico bag was produced, and in this bag, very carefully wrapped up in another rag, were several slices of a dried root, which the Indian informed me was very potent. I tasted it and found it to be the Indian turnip(*Arisæma*). Dr. Bigelow (Am. Med. Bot.) says "the root loses nearly all its acrimony by drying, and in a short time becomes quite inert." But this which the Indian showed me was intensely acrid, and it had been dried for several months. I have not seen the plant growing in this vicinity, but if it is not a different variety from the eastern species, it certainly retains its potency for a much longer period.

The Indians have shown me at different times other plants which they said were good for certain complaints, but I have never seen them exhibited as medicine. It is to be observed, however, that there is scarcely an herb of any kind which grows on the Cape or its vicinity, but is considered a medicine in the hands of some one or other, and so what one considers good another ridicules, for as they have no knowledge of the diagnosis of disease, they are apt to think that what is good in one case is good in all. Thus, one doctor acquired quite a reputation by administering a pasty mass composed of the shell of the *Natica*, ground with water on a stone. This was useful in cases of acidity of the stomach arising from surfeits of butter and oil. Another tried the same remedy in the case of an abscess on the liver, but the patient died and the medicine was ridiculed. I think, as a general rule, they have but little confidence in their own preparations, as they invariably come to me after a trial of a day or two of their native remedies; and the whole of their materia medica is employed after the manner of the old women of all countries. But their ceremonials and tamánawas, and the manipulations and juggling feats of the doctor they have great faith in, and will probably continue them for a long time to come, if indeed they ever relinquish the practice.

Various plants have been shown me by the Indians as valuable during parturition, but I do not think they are in general use. As a rule the Indian women require but little assistance during labor, and it is very rare that one dies during childbirth. I saw an instance of one who was taken with labor pains while on her way to the brook for water. This was a very unusual occurrence, as they generally keep in the house at such times. My attention was called to the circumstance by seeing her sitting on the ground and another squaw supporting her back. I went out to learn the cause, and found that she had just been delivered of a child. The woman sat still for a few moments longer, then got up and walked into the house without assistance. They are seldom confined to the house over a day, and often not over a couple of hours. That the process is somewhat shorter, and apparently attended with less suffering than among white women, is probably owing to a much lower degree of nervous sensibility, rather than to any material physical difference. The children are, as a usual thing, well formed. I have heard of cases of malformation, but during three years past have not seen a single one. Twins are of rare occurrence, and during the same period I knew of but one instance, which happened on Tattoosh Island during the summer of 1864. The Indians did not seem to know what to do about it. They considered it as a sort of evil which would affect in some way the summer fisheries. So the woman and her husband were sent back to Neeah Bay, and prohibited from eating fish of any description for two or three months; and had it not been for the food procured at the Agency she must have starved. The twins died shortly after their birth, and I strongly suspect that they were killed by the Indians to get rid of the demons which were supposed to have come with them.[1]

In cases of sickness where the doctors consider that the patient cannot recover, it was formerly the custom to turn the sufferer out of doors to die, particularly if it was something they did not understand; the belief being, that if suffered to die in a house all the other occupants would die of the same disease. An instance came under my observation of a woman who was paralyzed so as to be utterly helpless. They dragged her out upon the beach on a cold wintry day, and left her on the snow to perish. The sympathies of the white residents were aroused, and several Indians were appealed to to take the woman into their lodges, and payment offered them for the performance of this simple act of humanity; but all refused through fear. They were, however, finally induced by promise of reward, and with the assistance of myself and another white person, to construct a rude hovel, in which she was placed, and food and fuel supplied her; but the Indians would do nothing more, and she was attended by the white residents and made as comfortable as the circumstances would admit, until death relieved her. Since then, and for the past two years, no instances of like inhumanity have occurred; the Indians fearing lest the agent would punish them for a repetition of the offence. But I have been frequently assured that, except for this, they would have treated several other patients in a similar manner.

---

[1] The same superstition exists among other tribes. Some years ago a woman belonging to a party who were being conveyed on a California river steamer to their reservation, gave birth to twins, which were immediately thrown overboard.—G. G.

FUNERAL CEREMONIES.—When a person dies the body is immediately rolled up in blankets and firmly bound with ropes and cords, then doubled up into the smallest possible compass and placed in a box which is also firmly secured with ropes. When all is ready, the boards of a portion of the roof are removed, and the box with the body taken out at the top of the house and lowered to the ground, from a superstition that if a dead body is carried through the doorway, any person passing through it afterwards would sicken and die. The box is then removed to a short distance from the house, and sometimes placed in a tree; but of late years the prevailing custom is to bury it in the earth. A hole is first dug with sticks and shells deep enough to admit the box, leaving the top level with the surface. Boards are then set up perpendicularly all around so as to completely inclose it, their ends rising above the ground from four to five feet. A portion of the property of the deceased is placed on top of the box; this, in the case of a man, consists of his fishing or whaling gear, or a gun with the lock removed, his clothing, and bedding. If a female, beads and bracelets of brass, iron, calico, baskets, and her apparel. A little earth is thrown on top, and then the whole space filled up with stones. Blankets, calico, shawls, handkerchiefs, looking glasses, crockery and tin ware, are then placed around and on the grave for show, no particular order being observed, but each being arranged according to the fancy of the relatives of the deceased. The implements used in digging the grave are also left and placed among the other articles. A description of a few of these graves may not be out of place. One was that of a woman who was buried at Baäda, the eastern extremity of Neeah Bay. The husband was a young chief, who decorated it as became his ideas of his dignity. In front of the grave was a board on which was painted the representation of a rainbow, which they believe has great claws at each end with which it grasps any one so unfortunate as to come within its reach. On top of the board, which formed its edge, was a sort of shelf containing the crockery ware of the deceased; and on the left corner a carved head of an owl, wrapped up with a white cloth. A short stick wound with calico at the right corner bore a handkerchief at its top, and from two tall poles similarly wound around with calico a shawl, a dress pattern, and some red flannel were displayed like flags. At the expiration of a year the cloth disappeared, having been rotted by the rains and torn into shreds by the wind.

Another was the grave of a chief named Hure-tall, known by the whites as "Swell," and who was killed by an Elwha Indian in 1861 while engaged in bringing supplies from Port Townsend for the trading post at Neeah Bay. As he was an Indian well known and very much respected by the whites, his body was received by some settlers at Port Angeles, and placed in a box, and was brought from thence to Neeah Bay by a brother of the deceased, assisted by myself and another white man. The box was deposited in the ground, after the custom of the Indians, and over his remains a monument was raised by the relatives. It is built of cedar boards, and surmounted by a pole on the top of which is a tin oil can. Around its base are the painted tamánawas boards which he had in his lodge. A third grave is that of an Indian boy, at Baäda. A couple of posts were set up at the ends, and boards fastened to them which were covered with blankets. In the centre of the upper edge of the boards an eagle's tail was fastened, spread out like a fan; two guns without locks were hung up at the ends, and a stick with a piece of calico served as a streamer. All these graves, with the exception of Swell's, are now denuded of their covering of cloth, nothing being replaced when once destroyed by the elements.

The tying a corpse in its blanket is of recent date. Formerly it was not considered necessary to be so particular, but a case of suspended animation, where the patient recovered, having occurred some ten years ago, they adopted it to prevent any future instances of the same kind. The circumstance, as related to me by some Indians, is as follows: The Indian, whose name was Harshlah, resided at Baäda village, and died, or was supposed to have died, after a very brief illness. He was buried in the usual manner, but in two days after he managed to free himself and to make his appearance among his friends, greatly to their consternation. After having assured them that he was no spirit, but really alive, they were induced to listen to his statement. He said that he had been down to the centre of the earth, which the Indians suppose to be the abode of the departed, and there he saw his relatives and friends, who were seated in a large and comfortable lodge enjoying themselves. They told him that he smelled bad like the live people, and that he must not remain among them. So they sent him back. The people he saw there had no bones; these they had left behind them on the earth; all they had taken with them was their flesh and skin, which, as it gradually disappeared by decomposition after death, was removed every night to their new abode, and when all was carried there, it assumed the shape each one wore on earth. It is one of the avocations of the dead to visit the bodies of their friends who have died, and gradually, night by night, remove the flesh from the bones, and carry it to the great resting-place, the lodge in the centre of the earth. He further stated that on his return to where he had been buried he struggled and freed himself from his grave-cloth and the box, and then discovered that he had been dead.[1]

This man Harshlah afterwards died of small-pox, and my informant remarked that the second time he was tied up so securely that he never came to life again. Since then they have been very particular to secure all bodies so firmly that a revival is hopeless. This circumstance, so fresh in the minds of all the adults of the tribe, and the revelations respecting the other world, which correspond so exactly with their ancient ideas, make it impossible to teach them our views of a future state. They do not doubt the white man's statement, but they say that his heaven, which is represented to be in the sky, is not intended for the Indian, whose abode is in the earth. I have known several instances where, from the attending circumstances, there is little doubt that persons have been buried while in a swoon, or in a simply comatose state, and I have repeatedly urged upon them the folly of burying such persons before means could be tried to resuscitate them; but I never have been able to get them to wait a single moment after they think the breath

---

[1] Cases of apparent death, sometimes, perhaps, feigned for the purpose of acquiring influence, or notoriety, are not unfrequent among these coast tribes, and in all those I have known, a similar story has been told of a visit to the dead country.—G. G.

has left the body. On the 10th of October, 1864, Sierchy, a middle-aged man of general good health, was reported to me as having just died. It appeared that the evening previous he had eaten a raw carrot, which the farmer on the reservation had given him, and towards morning he complained of a pain in his breast, but as he made no request for assistance, his squaw took no notice of him, and at sunrise went about preparing the usual meal. While thus engaged, she noticed Sierchy to exhibit a slight convulsive motion, and as she supposed instantly die. She at once began to howl, and in this was joined by the rest of the squaws. I was sent for and went over to the lodge, which was only four or five rods from my quarters; but when I arrived, which could not have been over ten minutes from the time the man was supposed to have died, the others had wrapped him up in his blanket, and wound a stout cord tight around him from head to foot, drawing it so firmly about the neck that it would have suffocated a well person in five minutes. I tried to induce them to undo the face and let me attempt to restore him, for I thought he had only swooned away, or at the worst had but a fit from eating the carrot, which they had told me about, but I could not persuade them. "It was very bad to look on the face of the dead, and they must be covered from sight as soon as they cease to breathe." So they carried him out and buried him. I shall always, however, think that if proper means had been tried, he would have speedily revived. Another case was that of a squaw who had suddenly lost her husband a few days before. He had been sick for a long time and had apparently recovered; but taking a severe cold, he died from its effects in about twenty-four hours from the time of the attack. The woman was remarkably stout, and in good health. I saw her sitting by the bank of the brook, lamenting the death of her husband, and passed by to the upper village, about a quarter of a mile distance, where having attended some sick persons, I was about returning to the school building, when I heard the wailing cry of women announcing death. I quickened my steps and soon learned that it was the same woman I had passed but a short time previously, weeping for her husband, who was now also announced as dead. By the time I could get into the lodge, she too was tied up and in a box, ready to be buried, nor would the friends listen to a word I said, or permit me to use any measures for her recovery. Dead she was, they were sure, or if not, they took good means to insure that she should be so shortly.

As soon as an Indian dies the property, if there be any, is divided at once among the relations and friends. The time of mourning is one year, and at the expiration of the period, or on the return of the same season, or the same moon, the nearest surviving relative gives a feast and distributes presents, both to appease the spirit of the departed and to give notice that mourning is over. During the interval it is considered disrespectful to mention the name of the deceased in the hearing of relatives or friends, and whenever it is necessary to speak the name to a white person, it is invariably done in an undertone or whisper.

Although I have stated that it is the general custom to place the dead in a box, yet it is not the invariable practice, as, in case of persons of inferior rank who are either old or poor, it not unfrequently occurs that they are simply wrapped in a blanket and a mat and buried in the ground. The bodies of slaves are dragged a short distance from the lodge and covered over with a mat. In the case of the old man whom I mentioned in connection with the performance of the doctor, and whose body I assisted to bury, he was simply rolled in his blanket, lashed up firmly in a mat, and buried in a shallow grave. Over the remains were piled broken boxes, mats, old blankets, and the clothing he had worn. Care is always taken to render worthless everything left about a grave, so that the cupidity of the evil minded may not tempt them to rob the dead. Blankets are cut into strips, crockery ware is cracked or broken, and tin pans and kettles have holes punched through them.

No monuments of a lasting character mark the last resting place of even the greatest chief. Whatever of display there may be made at the time of burial is of an ephemeral nature calculated to last but for a year, and after that but little care or respect is shown the remains. As time elapses the graves go to decay, and the bones of the dead lie scattered around. During the clearing of land at Neeah Bay for the uses of the Agency a large number of bones and skulls were found, which were all gathered and burned, the sight of such relics of humanity being offensive to the feelings of the whites.

There are no antiquities connected with this tribe; such as earthworks, mounds, or other evidences of the usages of former generations. All that the antiquarian can find to repay him for his researches are arrow-heads of stone, and ancient daggers and hatchets of the same material, which are occasionally thrown up by the plough or occasionally found on the surface. The mounds of shells and other debris of ancient feasts are but the refuse of the lodges, and whatever may be found in them has not been so deposited from any design, but simply lost or thrown away. The only fortifications they have used as a defence against enemies were the rude stockades or pickets of poles, which I have before alluded to, and which have gradually decayed or have been used as firewood.

SUPERSTITIONS.—Besides the legends I have already related, there are others which may serve to convey an idea of the mental character of the tribe, and throw some light upon statements made by early explorers on the northwest coast. There is a remarkable rock standing detached from the cliff at the northwest extremity of the Cape, a little south of the passage between the main land and Tatoosh Island. This rock, the Indian name of which is Tsá-tsá-dak, rises like a pillar from the ocean over a hundred feet almost perpendicularly, leaning, however, a little to the northwest. Its base is irregular in form, and about sixty feet in diameter at its widest portion near the surface of the water. It decreases in size till at the top it is but a few yards across, and on its summit are low stunted bushes and grass. It is entirely inaccessible except on its southeastern side, where a person possessed of strength and nerve could, with great difficulty, ascend, but to get down by the same way would be impossible. The Indians have a tradition respecting this Pillar Rock, that many years ago an Indian climbed to its summit in search of young cormorants and gulls, which make it a resort during the breeding season; but after he had reached the top he could not again descend. All the attempts he made were fruitless, and at length his friends went to his relief, every expedient they could think of being resorted to without success. They tied strings to their arrows and tried to shoot them over, but they could not make them ascend sufficiently high. They caught gulls and fastened threads to their feet, and tried to make them fly over and draw the string across the rock, but all was of no avail. Six days were wasted in the vain attempt to save him, and on the seventh he lay down and died. His spirit, say the Indians, still lives upon the rock, and gives them warning when a storm is coming on, which will make it unsafe for them to go out to sea in pursuit of their usual avocations of killing whales or seals, or catching fish. Duncan, one of the early explorers, mentions this rock and gives a drawing of it, but he places it between the island and the main land. Vancouver, in alluding to Duncan's statement, says he saw no such rock. It does not exist where Duncan states he saw it, but it does exist about one mile a little east of south of Tatoosh Island. It is easily seen when sailing up the coast close in land; but when opposite to it at a short distance off it is so overtopped by the cliffs of the Cape as not to be particularly noticeable. The passage between the island and the main land is half a mile wide, and is not, as is stated by various authors, obstructed by a reef connecting the island and the cape, but has a depth of four and five fathoms of water through its entire distance; and although there are several rocks which are bare at low water, yet vessels can pass through at any stage of the tide, providing the wind is fair, for the ebb and flood tides rush through with great velocity, making tide rips which have been mistaken for shoals. I have passed through the passage in a schooner twice, and I know of several other vessels that have gone through without the slightest difficulty.

There is another rock not far from the Pillar Rock, near the top of which is a sort of cavity, across which rests a large spar which has been borne on the crest of some stupendous wave and tossed into its present resting place. It had been there long before the memory of the present generation of Indians, and is believed by them to have been placed there by supernatural agency, and is consequently regarded with superstitious awe. They think that any one who should attempt to climb up and dislodge it would instantly fall off the rock and be drowned. All down the coast from Cape Flattery to Point Grenville, pillar rocks are seen of various heights and sizes, and most fantastic shapes, and for each and all of them the Indians have a name and a traditionary legend. About midway between the cape and Flattery Rocks is one of these pillars, looking in the distance like a sloop with all sail set. The tide sets strongly round it both at flood and ebb. The Indians believe a spirit resides upon it, whose name is Se-kä-jee-ta, and to propitiate it, and give them a good wind and smooth sea, they throw overboard a small present of dried fish or any other food they may have whenever they pass by.

The aurora borealis they think is the light caused by the fires of a mannikin tribe of Indians who live near the north pole, and boil out blubber on the ice. On one occasion while in a canoe on the Strait of Fuca at night, there was a magnificent display of the aurora, and I asked the chief who had charge of the canoe, if he knew what it was. He said, far beyond north, many moons' journey, live a race of little Indians not taller than half the length of this paddle. They live on the ice and eat seals and whales. They are so strong that they dive into the water and catch whales with their hands, and the light we saw was from the fires of those little people boiling blubber. They were skookooms, and he did not dare speak their names.[1] Drowned persons they supposed to turn into owls, and several years since a party of Indians having been lost by the accidental demolishing of their canoe by the tail of a whale they were killing, I was gravely assured that the night after the accident eight owls were seen perched on the houses of the drowned men, and each had suspended from his bill the shell worn in the nose of the man while alive.

A most ludicrous instance of their superstition occurred while I was making a survey of the reservation during the summer of 1862. A chief, Kobetsi, who lived at Tsuess village, owned a large cranberry meadow, of the possession of which he was very jealous. Among the Indians who accompanied me on the survey was a young man who had quite recently had a difficulty with Kobetsi, in which he felt that the chief was the aggressor. The Indians, who are very fertile in inventing tales, informed Kobetsi that the fellow had sold the cranberry meadow to me, and that I had a great medicine which I could set in the field which would gather all the cranberries. This medicine was a field compass. They had seen the mariner's compass, but a field compass on a Jacob staff was something they could not comprehend. Old Kobetsi believed the tale, and sent a party, armed and painted, from the island where he was then residing, to attack me and the surveying party at Tsuess. We did not happen to be there on their arrival, so they returned; but the following day I went down and finished the survey, and after returning home the old chief, who had been informed of the fact, came himself from Tatoosh Island with his warriors to demand redress for the supposed loss of his cranberries. He was soon convinced of the real facts, and left, quite mortified that he had worked himself up into such a state of excitement about nothing; but he still believed that the compass possessed great and mysterious properties, and requested me not to place it on his land again. Another instance of superstition was during the time of my taking a census of the tribe in 1861. The Indians at Hosett village were much opposed to giving me their names, from the belief that every man, woman, or child whose names were entered in my book, would have the small-pox and die.

The cliffs at the extreme point of Cape Flattery are pierced by deep caverns and arches that admit the passage of canoes, not only saving the distance of going around or outside the rocks during rough weather, but affording snug coves and shelter during high wind, and secure passages for the Indian to skulk along unseen. Some of the caverns extend a great distance under the cliff, and afford hiding places for seals, which, however, are not allowed to remain always in peace; for the Indian, watching an opportunity when it is calm, boldly ventures in as far as his canoe can be managed; then with a torch in one hand, and a knife in the other, he dashes into the water and wades or swims to where the seals are lying on the sandy bottom at the remote end of the cave. The light partially blinding and stupefying the

---

[1] Traditions of the Eskimos as a race of dwarfs, possessing supernatural powers, who dwell in the "always night country," are current among the Indians of Puget Sound also. One of the incentives to desperate resistance by them during the war of 1855–56, was the circulation by their chiefs of a story that it was the intention of the whites to take them all there in a steamer. The idea of eternal cold and darkness carried with it indescribable horrors to their imaginations.—G. G.

animals, and the Indian, taking advantage of this, is enabled to kill as many as he can reach. But this is an exploit attended with great danger, for occasionally the torch will go out, and leave the cavern in the profoundest darkness. At such times the cries of the seals, mingled with the roar of the billows as it echoes through the caves, inspire the Indian with a mortal terror; and should he escape with his life, he will have most fearful tales to relate of the dark doings and still darker and mysterious sayings of the beings who are believed to inhabit these caverns and dens of the earth, and who being angry because their secret retreats were invaded, blew out the torch, and filled the air with the horrid sounds he heard. It is, however, but seldom that the usually turbulent waters in the vicinity of the cape are quiet enough to permit of such expeditions.

The craggy sides of the perpendicular cliffs afford resting places for numerous sea fowl, particularly the violet-green cormorant, which here builds its nest whereever it can find a hole left by some pebble or boulder fallen from the cliff, or where it can scratch or burrow into any loose soil that may form the summit. Harlequin ducks, mokes, guillemots, petrels and gulls abound, and during the breeding season the air is filled with their discordant cries. These birds are all considered as departed Indians, and the cries they utter in an approaching storm, are supposed to be warnings of dead friends not to venture around the cape till it shall have abated.

Lichens and moss collect on the sides of the cliffs above the direct action of the waves, and where the tides reach, the rocks are covered with barnacles and mussels, or else entirely hidden by sea-weeds which grow in rich profusion. In some places there are beds of clay slate in the conglomerate which have been bored full of holes by the borer clam (*Parapholas*), and present a singular appearance; elsewhere they are the resting places of a great variety of starfish, sea slugs, limpets, etc. Some of these to the Indian mind are great medicines, others of them are noxious, and some are used for food. The jutting promontories, the rocky islets, and detached boulders, the caverns and archways about the Cape have all some incident or legend, and in one large cave, opposite Tatoosh Island where the breakers make an unusual sound, which becomes fearful on the approaching of a storm, they think a demon lives, who, coming forth during the tempest, seizes upon any canoes that may be so unfortunate as to pass at the time, and takes them and their crews into the cave, from whence they issue forth as birds or animals, but never again in human shape. The grandeur of the scenery about Cape Flattery, and the strange contortions and fantastic shapes into which its cliffs have been thrown by some former convulsion of nature, or worn and abraded by the ceaseless surge of the waves; the wild and varied sounds which fill the air, from the dash of water into the caverns and fissures of the rocks, mingled with the living cries of innumerable fowl, the great waves of the ocean coming in with majestic roll and seemingly irresistible force, yet broken into foam, or thrown into the air in jets of spray, all combined, present an accumulation of sights and sounds sufficient to fill a less superstitious beholder than the Indian with mysterious awe.

The astronomical and meteorological ideas of the Makahs are wrapped in vague and mythological tales. Of the revolutions of the heavenly bodies they know nothing more than that the sun in summer is higher in the heavens than during the winter, and that its receding or approach causes the difference of cold and heat of the seasons. The stars are believed to be the spirits of Indians and representatives of every animal that has existed on earth, whether beast, bird, or fish. Their notions, however, are very confused, for as they think that all who die go immediately to the centre of the earth, they find it difficult to explain how they get from there to become luminaries in the sky.[1] Most, if not all the constellations have names, such as the whale, halibut, skate, shark, etc., but I have never had any of them pointed out to me; they seemed to have a superstitious repugnance to doing so, and although they will at times talk about the stars, they generally prefer cloudy weather for such conversations. The moon they believe is composed of a jelly-like substance, such as fishes eat. They think that eclipses are occasioned by a fish like the "cultus" cod, or toosh-kow, which attempts to eat the sun or moon, and which they strive to drive away by shouting, firing guns, and pounding with sticks upon the tops of their houses. On the 5th of December, 1862, I witnessed the total eclipse of the moon, and had an opportunity of observing their operations. There was a large party gathered that evening at the house of a chief who was giving a feast. I had informed some of the Indians during the day that there would be an eclipse that evening, but they paid no regard to what I said, and kept on with their feasting and dancing till nearly ten o'clock, at which time the eclipse had commenced. Some of them coming out of the lodge at the time, observed it and set up a howl, which soon called out all the rest, who commenced a fearful din. They told me that the toosh-kow were eating the moon, and if we did not drive them away they would eat it all up, and we should have no more. As the moon became more and more obscure, they increased their clamor, and finally, when totally obscured, they were in great excitement and fear. Thinking to give them some relief, I got out a small swivel, and with the assistance of one of the employés of the reservation, fired a couple of rounds. The noise, which was so much louder than any they could make, seemed to appease them, and as we shortly saw the silvery edge of the moon make its appearance after its obscuration, they were convinced that the swivel had driven off the toosh-kow before they had swallowed the last mouthful. I tried to explain the cause of the eclipse, but could gain no converts to the new belief, except one or two who had heard me explain and predict the eclipse during the previous day, and who thought as I could foretell so correctly what was going to take place, I could also account for the cause.

Their idea of the aurora borealis I have already explained. Comets and meteors are supposed to be spirits of departed chiefs. Rainbows are supposed to be of a malignant nature, having some connection with the Thlookloots, or Thunder Bird,

---

[1] I believe that this may be explained: the stars are the spirits of the pre-human and not of the existing race. Almost all nations have given the names of animals to certain constellations; thus the Eskimo call the Great Bear the Cariboo, the Puget Sound Indians call it the Elk, etc.—G. G.

and to be armed at each end with powerful claws with which to grasp any unhappy person who may come within their reach.

Of time they keep but little record. They have names for the different months or moons, twelve of which constitute with them two periods, the warm and cold. They can remember and speak of a few days or a few months, but of years, according to our computation, they know nothing. Their "year" consists of six months or moons, and is termed *tsark-wark it-chie*. The first of these periods commences in December, when the days begin to lengthen, and continues until June. Then, as the sun recedes and the days shorten, another commences and lasts till the shortest days. It is owing to the fact of these periods being only six months in duration, that it is so difficult for them to tell their ages according to our estimate, for as their knowledge of counting is very limited, they cannot be made to understand our reckoning. I have never known them to remember the proper age of a child of over two years. Sometimes they give the age of an individual by connecting his birth with some remarkable event, as, for instance, the year of the smallpox, or when a white man came to reside among them, or that when a vessel was wrecked.

The seasons are recognized by them as they are by ourselves, namely, spring, by the name of klairk-shiltl; summer, by that of kla-pairtch; autumn, by kwi-atch; and winter, by wake-puett.

The names of the months are as follows:—

December is called se-hwow-as-put'hl, or the moon in which the se-whow, or cheta-pook, the California gray whale, makes its appearance.

January is a-a-kwis-put'hl, or the moon in which the whale has its young.

February, kluk-lo-chis-to-put'hl, or the moon when the weather begins to grow better and the days are longer, and when the women begin to venture out in canoes after firewood without the men.

March is named o-o-lukh-put'hl, or the moon when the finback whales arrive.

April, ko-kose-kar-dis-put'hl. The moon of sprouts and buds.

May, kar-kwush-put'hl. Moon of the strawberry and "salmon berry."

June, hay-sairk-toke-put'hl. The moon of the red huckleberry.

July is kar-ke-sup-he-put'hl, or the moon of the wild currants, gooseberry, and sallal, *Gaultheria*.

August is wee-kookh, or season of rest; no fish taken or berries picked, except occasionally by the children or idle persons; but it is considered by the tribe as a season of repose.

September is kars-put'hl, when all kinds of work commence, particularly cutting wood, splitting out boards, and making canoes.

October, or kwar-te-put'hl, is the moon for catching the tsa-tar-wha, a variety of rockfish, which is done by means of a trolling line with a bladder buoy at each end, and a number of hooks attached.

November is called cha-kairsh-put'hl, or the season of winds and screaming birds.

The terminal put'hl seems to be equivalent to our word "season," for although the words to which it is added signify but one moon, yet when speaking of a month's duration the word dah-kah is used, as tsark-wark dah-kah, one month.

Daylight or daytime is expressed by the word Klc-se-hark, which also means sun; but in enumerating days the word che-al'th is used, denoting a day and night, or twenty-four hours; thus, tsark-wark che-al'th, one day, &c. The divisions of the day are sunrise, yó-wie; noon, ta-kus'-sie; sunset, art'hl-há-chitl; evening, ar-tuktl; midnight, up'ht-ut-haie.

Wind is called wake-sie; the north wind, batl-et-tis; the south, kwart-see-die; the east, too-tooch-ah-kook; the southeast, too-chee; the west, wa-shel-lie, and the northwest yu-yoke-sis. These are each the breath of a fabulous being who resides in the quarter whence the wind comes, and whose name it bears.

Kwartseedie, the south wind, brings rain,[1] and the cause of it is this: Once upon a time the Mouse, the Flounder, the Cuttlefish, the Skate, with several other fishes and some land animals, resolved to visit Kwartseedie and see how he lived. After a journey of many days they found him asleep in his house, and thought they would frighten him; so the Cuttlefish got under the bed, the Flounder and Skate lay flat on the floor, and the other visitors disposed themselves as they thought best. The Mouse then jumped on the bed and bit Kwartseedie's nose, which suddenly awakened him; and as he stepped out of bed he slipped down by treading on the Flounder and Skate, while the Cuttlefish, twining round his legs, held him fast. This so enraged him that he began to blow with such force that the perspiration rolled down from his forehead in drops and formed rain. He finally blew all his tormentors home again; but he never has forgotten the insult, and comes at intervals to annoy his enemies, for the land animals at such times are very uncomfortable, and the fish are driven from their feeding grounds on the shoals by the great breakers, which also oftentimes throw vast numbers of them on shore to perish.

The legends respecting all the other winds are very similar, and their blowing is a sign of the displeasure of their imaginary beings.

The Indians are excellent judges of the weather, and can predict a storm or calm with almost the accuracy of a barometer. On a clear calm night, if the stars twinkle brightly they expect strong wind, but if there is but a slight scintillation they are certain of a light wind or a calm, and consequently will start at midnight for the fishing grounds, fifteen or twenty miles due westward from Cape Flattery, where they remain till the afternoon of the following day. Their skill is not surprising when it is understood that their time is in great measure passed upon the water, on a most rugged coast; that their only means of travel is by canoes, and that from childhood up it is as natural for them to watch the weather as it is for a sailor on the ocean to note the sky.

---

[1] It is the prevalent winter wind of the northwest coast.—G. G.

MAKAH VOCABULARY.[1]

A

Above; or over head, (when spoken of things in a house.)	*ha-dás-suk.*
Above; up high (expression used out of doors.)	*ha-tárts-tl.*
Aboard	*hay-túks.*
go on board	*hay-túks-ill.*
it is on board	*hay-tuks-uk.*
Across; as to cross a stream	*kwit-swar-tis.*
Afraid	*win'natch.*
After	*wà-hark.*
Agreeable or pleasant, to taste or smell	{ *cháb-bas* or *chám-mas.*
Again	*kláo.*
give me again	*klao-káh.*
Another or other	*klá-oukh.*
Another; personal	*do-wá-do.*
Alive	*tee-chée.*
All	*dobc.*
Always	*kay-uttl.*
Angry	*koh-sap'h.*
Ankle	*kul-lá-kul-lie.*
Arrive at, to	*wart-luk.*
When did you arrive at Victoria?	*ardis chealth kwiksa wartluk Bictolia.*
When did you arrive home?	*ardis chealth kwiksa ut-sáie.*
Arms	*wak-sas.*
right arm	*chah-bát-sas.*
left arm	*kart-sar.*
Arrow	*tsa-hút-chitl,* or *tsa-hat-tie.*
Arrow-head, of wood	*tsá-tsuk-ta-kwillh.*
of bone	*hah-sháh-biss.*
of iron	*chee-chair-kwillh.*
Autumn	*kwiatch.*
Axe	*he-sée-ak.*

B

Back, the	*hey-túks-uthl.*
Bad	*klay-ass.*
Bag or sack	*klar-airsh.*
Barberry (berberis oregoniensis)	*klook-shitl-ko-bupt.*
Barbs of harpoon	*tsa-kwat.*
Bark	*tsar-kar-bis.*
Barrel	*bat-lap-tl.*
Barnacle	*kléep-é-hud.*
Bat	*thlo-thle-kwok-e-batl.*
Battledore, or boy's bat	*klá-hairk.*
Basket	*bo-whie.*
little basket	*pe-koe.*
Beach	*sis-sá-bits.*
Beads	*cluk-partl-shitl.*
large cut beads	*kar-kwap-pah.*
Behind	*o-uk'-atl.*
Berries	*hoats-ak-tup.*
ripe berries	*sa-kátch-tl.*
to gather berries	*chi-ark.*
Birds (generic)	*hooke-toop.*
young birds	*de-dak-tl.*
sea ducks	*ko-whaithl.*
cormorant (graceulus violaceus)	*klo-poise.*
crane	*kwar-less.*
crow	*char-kar-do.*
butter duck	*chish-kul-ly.*

[1 In the Makah, as in all the languages of this part of the Western Coast, the letters *r*, *f*, and *v* are wanting; as also *th*, whether hard or soft. Mr. Swan has employed the *r* following the vowel *a* to indicate the Italian sound, as in *father*, and after *ai*, &c., to represent the neuter vowel *u*, as in the English *but*, and the French *je*. The letter *r* in pronouncing English words is changed to *b* or *m*. These last are convertible letters, as are also *d* and *n*. *Th*, when it occurs in the text or the vocabulary, is to be understood as an aspirated *t*, as in the French *thé* —G. G.]

(93)

94   THE INDIANS OF CAPE FLATTERY.

Birds		Body, *parts of*	
mallard duck	dah-hah-tich.	hand	klar-klar-he-do-koob.
surf duck	al-ló-hain.	fingers	tsar-tsár-kwle-de-koob.
harlequin duck	tsat-tsowl-chak.	thumb	bä-bä-bits-ä-de-koob.
scaup duck	ko-ho-ash.	nails	chath-latcht.
eagle, bald	ar-kwár-tid.	breast or chest	hćy-dus-hothl.
eagle, golden	kwa-kwát-i-buks.	woman's bosom	a-dab.
goose	hah-dikh.	back	hä-tuks-itl.
guillemot	klo-klo-chuh-sooh.	leg	klä-ish-chid.
gulls	kwá-lil.	ankle	kul-la-kully.
grebe (*Podiceps occidentalis*)	ah-low-ah-háiu.	foot	klar-klar-tsoob.
		toes	tsark-tsark-itl-sub.
grouse	too-too-artsh.	bones	hah-shah-biss.
heron	hah-to-bad-die.	heart	chah-pah or kle-buks-tie.
humming-bird	kwe-tá-kootch.	blood	klar-klar-wá'rk-a-bus.
jay	kwish-kwish-ee.	liver	pil-lok.
kingfisher	chesh-kully.	fat or tallow	hä-biks.
pigeon, *band-tailed*	háy-nib.	kidney	atsh-pohb.
raven	klook-shood.	bladder	kal-läh-tah-chib.
woodpecker, *red-headed*	kta-kla-bethl-putch.	stomach	koo-you.
woodpecker, *golden-winged*	kle-haib.	belly	ko-só-ar-ty.
		intestines	tse-keup.
sandpiper	ho-hope-sis.	skin	klä-hark'.
oyster-catcher	kwe-kwe-aph.	penis	che-war.
Black	toop-kooh.	pudenda (female)	jude.
Blanket	hey-taid.	testes	kar-ko-bits.
blue blanket	art-lartl.	*swelled or enlarged testes*	dä-uk-tl.
red blanket	klä-har-thl.		
white blanket	kle-sethl.	**Boil,** *to*	klo-báhk-st.
green blanket	kor-buk-athl.	**Bone**	hah-shah-biss.
Blood	klar-klar-wárk-a-bus.	**Bore a hole,** *to*	tsćet-kä-tsit.
Blue	kwish'-kwish-á-kartl.	**Both**	dobe.
Board	klo-ailth.	**Bottle**	chah-bát-sits.
Body	chath-leet.	**Bow**	bis-tat-tie.
Body, *parts of*		**Bowstring**	tsee-tsits-see-dub.
head	to-hote-sid.	**Boy**	wik-we-ak.
hair, *on head*	app-sahp.	**Bracelets**	klar-klár-do-whas.
hair, *on body*	chee-pee.	**Break** or **destroy**	kokh-shitl.
face	hä-túk-witl.	**Breasts of woman**	a-dab.
face, handsome woman	klootlh-sooh hä-túk-witl.	**Bring,** *to*	o-hóse.
face, handsome man	kloo-klo hä-túk-witl.	**Broad** or **wide**	klo-ko.
forehead	hä-tuk-ant.	**Brother**	
ear	pay-paer.	elder	tak-ke-ai.
eye	kóllay.	younger	kar-thlatl-ik.
nose	choo-oáth-tl-tub.	**Bucket** or **box** for	
mouth	hä-tárks-tl.	carrying water	hoot-uts.
tongue	la-kairk.	**Buy,** *to*	bar-kuáll.
teeth	chee-chee.	**Burying-ground**	pćets-uks-sie.
beard	hah-puks'-ub.	**By** and **by**	ar-déei.
neck	tse-kwár-bits.	**Bread,** *soft*	llay-tlay-skook.
shoulder	hey-dah-kwitl.	*ship bread or hard biscuit*	ar-hósh-kook.
arm	wah-sas.		
elbow	hä-dah-park-tl.	**Buttons**	hoop-sooelth.
wrists	he-he-diár-kwe-douk.	**Butter**	tlat-say.

THE INDIANS OF CAPE FLATTERY. 95

C

Canoe, Chienook pat-
tern *chap-ats.*
large size for whaling,
to carry eight men *pah-dow-thl.*
medium size, to carry
six men *bó-kwis-tat.*
small size, to carry two
to four persons *ar-tlis-tat.*
very small, to carry one
person *ta-kaów-dah.*

(The whaling canoes are divided by thwarts or stretchers
into five compartments, which
are named as follows, as are
also the occupants :—)

the bow *hey-tuks-wad.*
the next behind *kah-kai-woks.*
centre of canoe *chah-thluk-do-as.*
the next behind *hey-tuk-stas.*
stern *klee-chah*
Candle, lamp, or
torch *la-kar-joss.*
Carry, *to* *há-dáiks.*
Carpenter, worker in
wood *kar-sár-kuk-tl.*
Calico for woman's dress *hah-dah-kwits.*
Catch, *to* *tsoo-kwitl.*
Cattle *boos-a-boos* or *moos-a-moos* (borrowed).
Cedar-bark *pret-sup.*
Chair *ko-kóke-we-dook* or *ta-kwát-ses.*
Chest or breast *hey-dus-ho-thl.*
Chest or box *klá-he-dethl* or *ar-hwe-dooks.*
Chisel for making canoes *klar-kar-yuk.*
Chicken-pox *yah-bass.*
Chief *cha-báth.*
Child *yá-duk.*
infant *ya-duk-kow-i-chee.*
Chop, *to* *he-sis.*
Clams (generic) *cha-its.*
qua-hang *cha-its.*
large clams (*Lutraria*) *har-loe.*
blue striated *har-ar-thlup.*
Clouds *kle-deek-a-bus.*
Coat *sa-se-tuk-lee.*
Cock *ahá-hah-cha-kope.*
Cockle *kla-lab.*
Codfish, *true* *kár-dartl.*

Codfish (a variety called
in the jargon *cultus*
cod) *toosh-ków.*
Codfish, *black* *be-showe.*
Cold, *I am*
cold weather *che-teer-hus.*
bat-lathl.
Colors
white *kle-sook.*
red *klay-hoke.*
black *toop-kook.*
blue, dark *toop-kook.*
blue, light *bo-kobe.*
green *kwar-buk-uk.*
Comb *kle-pe-ak.*
Common person *mis-che-mas* or *bis-che-bas.*
Come, *to* *ut-sai-ee.*
I come *ut-sai-atl-shie.*
you come *shoo-oógh.*
Contempt, *expression*
of
to a male *ká-shook.*
to a female *hey-hook.*
Cook, on stones *tá-chope.*
Copulate *koo-look.*
Corpse *kok-shitl.*
Cougar *hay-acd.*
Cough *wa'-wa-se-koss.*
Cradle *ya-duk-spa-tie.*
Crab (generic) *hol-lo-wah.*
Cranberries *pap-pas.*
Crane *kwar-less.*
Crow *cha-kár-do.*
Crooked *wake-iss-soo-its.*
Cry, *to* *kay-hark.*
Cup *tsiar-koob.*
Cut *kart-sap.*
Cuttlefish *te-thlope.*

D

Dance, *to* *hóth-look.*
Darkness *wis-tá-huk.*
Daughter (child) *har-dów-e-chuk.*
Day *kle-sé-hark.*
(This also means daylight.
In enumerating days, the
word *chealth* is used.)
Dead *kok-shal.*
Deadland (country of
the dead) *hay-tár-puthl.*
Deep *har-chee.*
Deer *bo-kwitch.*

96   THE INDIANS OF CAPE FLATTERY.

Demons (the primal race)	*che-che-wuptl.*	Feathers	*shoo-hóobe.*
devils	*ché-war.*	quills	*ki-thlă-id.*
Dig, to	*tsar-kwar-kethl.*	down	*pó-koke.*
Dirt	*sar-kwák-ă-bus.*	Fence	*klar-kub.*
Do, to	*bar-bóo-ak.*	Fight, to	*be-tŭk-we-dook.*
Dog	*keh-deitl.*	Find, to	*soo-kwartl.*
Dogfish	*yáh-chah.*	Finish, I have finished	
Door	*boo-shoo-i-sub.*	work or eating	*he-ártl.*
Down, bird's	*pó-hoke.*	File	*tee-chair-uk.*
Down stream	*ik-tar-wárk-liss*	Fingers	*tsar-tsar-kwle-de-koob.*
Dream, to	*o-oár-portl.*	Finger-ring	*kar-kar-buk-e-dóo-kup.*
Drink, I	*hoo-tuks-itl.*	Fir-tree	*sah-bah-tah-há-ko-buptl.*
Drive, to	*a-aiks or aáh-cks.*	Fire	*ah-dahk.*
Drunk	*a-whatl-youk.*	make fire	*ah-dáhk-sa.*
Dry	*klo-shówe.*	get up and make a fire	*koo-dook-shitl-ah-dahk-sa.*
Duck, mallard	*dah-hah-tich.*		
Dull	*wee-we-thuk-tl.*	Firewood	*ar-tik-sáh.*
Dung	*shab.*	First or before	*o-oltht.*
to dung	*shab-bah.*	Fish, to	*o-oash-taytl.*
		Fish	

E

Ear	*pă-páer.*
Earth	*kwe-che-ar.*
dirt	*sar-kwák-a-bus.*
Eagle, bald	*ar-kwár-tid.*
osprey	*kwa-kwal-i-buks.*
Eat	*hah-ouk.*
Echinus (sea-urchin)	
large	*toot-sup.*
small	*koats-kappr.*
Eggs	*dóo-chak.*
Eight	*ar-tles-sub.*
Elbow	*hă-dah-park-tl.*
Elk	*tóo-suk.*
End (or point)	*yu-chil-tish.*
Evening	*ar-tuk-tl*
Eye	*kollay.*
Exchange, to	*hó-oe-yah.*

(There is no generic name for fish; but when going for fish, the species are designated; for instance, for halibut, *o-oash-taytl-shoo-youtl*; for codfish, *o-oash-taytl-kardartl*, &c.)

brook trout	*klar-klek-tso.*
codfish, true	*kar-dar-tl.*
cod, false	*toosh-kow.*
cod, black	*be-shówe.*
red rockfish, or grouper	*klă-háp-pahr.*
black or mottled rockfish	*tsă-bár-whar.*
catfish (*Porichthys notatus*)	*ă-o-wit.*
dogfish	*yah-chah.*
flounder	*klu-klu-bais.*
flounder, large spotted	*kar-láthl-choo.*
halibut	*shoo-youtl.*
herring	*kloo-soob.*
salmon, spring or silver	*tsoo-wit.*
salmon, young	*tsow-thl.*
salmon, summer	*háh-dib.*
salmon, dog-tooth or fall	*cheech-kó-wis.*
salmon trout	*hópe-id* or *ho-péd.*
sapphire perch (embiotoca perspicabilis)	*wa-ă-kupt.*
sculpin, buffalo	*kab-biss.*
sculpin, large	*tsa-dairtch.*

F

Face	*hă-tuk-witl.*
Far	*táh-ness.*
Fat or fleshy, applied to persons	*ă-kŭ-ko-shee.*
Father	*do-waks.*
grandfather	*dar-dairks.*
Fathom	*ailtsh.*
one fathom	*tsark-we-ailtsh.*
two fathoms	*art-lailtsh.*
three fathoms	*wee-ailtsh.*
four fathoms	*bo-ailtsh*, &c.

THE INDIANS OF CAPE FLATTERY. 97

Fish	bit-la-chie.
shark	sah-bass.
Fish-club, *for killing fish*	tine-thl.
Fish-gig	heche-tl-tah.
Fish-hook	koo-yak.
halibut-hook	che-bood
barb of halibut-hook	kóo-sub.
wood of halibut-hook	tsar-whár-to-wik.
Fishing-line of kelp	sar-dat-tlh.
Fish-weir	boo-shóo-wah.
Five	sheutche.
Flea	bat-cha-seed.
Flesh	bret-sie.
Flounder, flatfish	klu-ktu-bais.
Flour	tlik-tlay-skoop.
Fly, *the insect*	bats-k'wad.
Food	har-ouk.
Foolish	a-whatl-tsuck.
drunk	a-whatl-youk.
Foot	kla-ish-ted or klar-dark-sub.
Forehead	há-tuks-aht.
Four	boh.
Formerly or a long time ago	hó-ái.
Freckled	joke-see.
Friend	yár-kwe-dook-uks.
Fry-pan	soo-uk-itl.
Full	tsar-bar

G

Gamble, *to*	húl-láh-ah.
to win at gambling	há-tarp.
to lose at gambling	há-lá-itl
Gambling-disks the wood from which the disks are made, a species of hazel	la-hullum. hul-iár-ko-bupt.
Get up, *to*	koo-dóok-shitl.
Get, *to*, or **receive**	tsóo-kwitl.
Girl	har-dów-e-chuk.
Give, *to*	klá-kase.
Go, *to*	klark-shitl.
I go	he-de-ár-saiks.
you go, *spoken to one*	he-de-ar-sitl-gie.
you go, *spoken to a number*	he-de-ar-sitl-chik.
one of you go	ar-dé-siche har-du-ass.
go quick	wá-háh-tte-gie â-á' -shie.
go along	wa-hoh-tle-gie.

13 January, 1870.

Go	
I go to the house	wättle-shaiks
I am going	wattle-she-áitl.
Good-bye	á-kiúh-lik-kar.
Good	klou-klo or klo-shish.
very good	kwar-ces-sar.
Goose	hár-duk or háh-dikh.
Grandfather	dá-dairks.
Grandmother	dá-dairks.
Grave, *a*	peets-uk-sie.
Grass	klar-kúpt.
Grain, growing	á-hósh-ko-bupt.
Grease	tlair-bass.
tallow	há-biks.
oil	kár-took.
Grebe (*Podiceps*)	á-low-ah-hain.
Green	kwar-búk-uk.
Grind, *to*	teh-chár-shitl.
Grouse	too-too-artsh.
Guillemot	klo-klo-chük-sook.
Gull	wha-lil or kwa-lil.
Gum or **pitch**	kluk-áit-a-bis.
Gun, double barrel single barrel, with flint lock	artl-dooh. poo-yah
single barrel, with percussion lock	hah-kul-la-kubtl.

H

Hail	kart-see-die.
Hair	ahp-sahp.
Haikwa (the dentalium)	che-lá-dook.
Half	yóoh-tah-dit-tait-so.
Halibut	shoo-youtl.
halibut-hook	che-bood.
Hand	klar-klar-he-do-koob.
right	char-bat-sas.
left	kart-sar.
left-handed	kart-sook.
Hands	to-la-pic.
Hard or **tough**	kar-tark.
Hare, *rabbit*	too-toop-jis.
Haul, *to*	cheatl.
haul canoe	cheatl-cha-pats.
portage for hauling canoes	cheatl-tar-shee.
Hawk	tast-át-wik.
Hat	se-ke-áh-poks.
Hay	klar-kupt.
He, when present	o-hok.
if absent	o-hoh.
Head	to-hóte-sid.

THE INDIANS OF CAPE FLATTERY.

English	Makah
Head-dress of dentalium, worn by young girls	batl-kup-klä-o-koob.
Hear	dah-áhh.
Heart	cháh-páh.
Hen	ah-hah-ha hai-up.
Here, *I am*	yath-tláy-ad.
Here	tec.
Heron	háh-to-bad-die.
Herring	k loo-sóob.
Hide, *to*	úptah.
Hit, *I*	há-pórp.
Hole	kó-we-tar.
Holla	hŭ'hh-shitl.
Hog	k lä-k lä-k war-tiltl.
How many	ár-dis.
Hoe	e-táks-darp.
House	ba-as.
Hundred	k lä-hó-oke or sheutch-e-uk.
Hungry	hár-koh.
are you hungry	hár-koh-kuk.
I am hungry	hár-koh-huss.
Husband	chä-kope.
Hurry, make haste	ä-ä-shic.

I

English	Makah
I	sé-ir.
Ice	koo-hooh.
Indians, *people*	k leits-ä-kwad-dic.
Infant	ya-duk-kow-it-chie or ya-tluk-kwa-ow-i-chuh.
Iron	k lair-yuh.
Island	oper-jec-ta.

J

English	Makah
Jay	k wish-kwish-shée.
Just now	k luh.
Jest, *to*, or a jesting person	tlá-tla-wik.

K

English	Makah
Kamass (*Scilla esculenta*)	kwad-dis or kwa-niss.
Kettle or pot	o-páh-suk.
Key	tluk-tlairk.
Kill, *to*	kokh-saph.
Knee	ko-ko-shák-le-de-koob.
Knee-pan	k lu-thlúk-le-de-koob.
Knife, sheath	kar-kairk.
pocket	kar-kairk.
dagger	to-kwark.
for splitting halibut	kó-che-tin.
Know, *I*	kum-ber-tups se-ir.
I don't know, or perhaps, or implying a doubt	kwóws.

L

English	Makah
Lake	chä-uk-tsope.
Large, great	ä-ä'-ho.
Lately, just now	k luh.
Laugh, *to*	k le-war.
Lazy	wee-wa-i.
I am lazy	wee-wä-i thluk-ä-thlits.
you are lazy	wee-wa-i thluk-a-thlus.
Leaf	k lä-kupt.
Leap	á-its-kutch.
Left, *the*	kart-sass.
left-handed	kart-sook.
Leg	k lä-ish-chid
Lice	kä-cheed.
nits or eggs of lice	karts-ar-kleed.
Lie, *to;* a falsehood	ká'-tah-bat-soot.
Light	dah-chówtl.
day-dawn	you-oui.
Lightning	kä-káirtch.
Like, similar	o-bobe-te.
Listen	dah-áhh.
Lively, spry	háh-háhts-tzae.
Long	há-ä-tse.
long time	kail-chiltl.
Look! to call the attention	k led-da.
Look for, *to*	dä-däh-chu-chish.
look here	har-dássie.
Love, *to*	yáh-ah-kups.
Low tide	k lu-shów-a-chish-chuck.
high tide	tsu-bä-i-chish-chuk.
Lynx	
Looking-glass	dah-chówtl.
Lose, *to*	cesh-sap.

M

English	Makah
Mallard duck	dah-hah-tih.
Mammals	
bat	thle-thle-kwok-e-battl.
bear, black	árt-leit-kwitl.

THE INDIANS OF CAPE FLATTERY. 99

Mammals		Miss	
beaver	de-hai-choo.	a mark, to	wake-tuch-e-dook.
cougar	há-aéd.	miss the road	wee-kuttl-shishtar-shee.
deer	bo-kwitch.	mistake in speech	ká-tárk-tish.
dog	keh-déitl.	**Molasses**	chám-o-set.
elk (*C. Canadensis*)	too-suk.	**Mole**	took-took-sh.
hare, *rabbit*	too-toop-jis.	**Mollusks**	
mink	kwár-tic.	barnacle	kle-bc-húd.
mole	took-took-sh.	clams	
mouse	se-bit-sa-bce.	large (*lutraria*)	har-loe.
land-otter	kar-to-wee.	blue striated	har-ar-thlup.
sea-otter	tee-juk.	cockle	klá-lab.
sea-lion	ar-kar-wad-dish.	haikwa (*dentalium*)	che-téh-dook.
seal (hair)	kars-chowce.	mussel	klo-chab.
seal (fur)	káith-la-dose.	oyster	kloh-kloh.
skunk	c-ail-á-hai-use.	thorn oyster	ko-okh-sá-de-buts.
squirrel	se-bi-to-wie.	scallop, large	klá-er-kwa-tie.
wolf	choo-choo-hu-wistl.	small	wad-dish.
whale (generic)	chét-á-pook.	sea-egg	koats-kapphr.
sperm	koats-kay.	**Month**	dah-kah.
right	yúch-yo-bad-die.	**Months**, names of	
fin-back	kow-wid.	January	a-a-kwis-puthl.
blackfish	klos-ko-kopphr.	February	klo-k'lo-chis-puthl.
sulphur-bottom	kwa-kwow-yák-thle.	March	o-o-tukh-puthl.
killer	che-che-wid.	April	ko-kose-kar-dis-puthl.
California gray	se-whoor or chet-a-pook.	May	kar-kwush-puthl.
porpoise	ár-ich-pethl.	June	hă-sairk-toke-puthl.
puffing pig	tsailth-ko.	July	kar-ke-supphr-puthl.
white-fin porpoise	kwar-kwartl.	August	wee-kooth.
Man	cha-kope.	September	kars-puthl.
young man	kla-hoke-she-thlar-sad.	October	kwar-te-puthl.
old man	ai-choob-e-chul.	November	chă-kairsh-puthl.
Many, *how*	ar-dis-ailth.	December	se-whow-ah-puthl.
Masks used in ceremonies	hooh-ków-itl-ik.	(The year consists of six months, and is called *tsarkwark-itchie*.)	
Mat of cedar-bark	bak-lap.		
large mat	kla-hairlt.	**Moon**	dah-kah.
small mat	che-bat.	**More**	tah-kah.
rush mat	to-dahh.	**Morning**	yóo-ie.
Meat, *fresh*	bect-sie.	**Mosquito**	wah-háts-tl.
Medicine	ko-ie or kow-ie.	**Mother**, *my*	a-bairks.
Medicine man, magician, or doctor	oash-tá-kay.	**Mountain**	hai-airch.
Medicine performances	tsi-ark.	**Mouse**	se-bit-sa-bce.
Medicine or tamanawas ceremonies	{ du-kwally or klook-wally.	**Mouth** .	há-tarks-tl.
Middle or **midway**	ah-pów-wad.	**Moxa**, a small cone of combustible matter burnt slowly in contact with the skin, to produce an eschar	bóo-chitl.
Milk	adab.		
Mill	chit-chit.		
Mind, *the*		(The inner bark of the white pine is used for the purpose.)	
male	kla-buks-tie.		
female	ha-dáh-dittl.	**Music** or **bell-ringing**	tsar-sik-sap.
Mink	kwar-tie.		

THE INDIANS OF CAPE FLATTERY.

Mussel	klo-chab.	**Numerals**	
My house	seir-bass.	11	tsark-woke.
My sister	klo-chuk-sub.	12	ut-tlai-ouk.
My things	ko-kote-sa-kut-liks.	13	wee-ouk.
Mythology	ho-hó-e-up or ho-ho-e-up-béss.	14	boh-kwe-ouk
(Names of two fabulous men of antiquity who changed men into animals, trees, and stones.)		15	sheutch-e-ouk.
		16	cheh-pártl-ouk.
		17	artl-pook.
		18	ar-tles-sub-ouk
		19	sar-kwas-sub-tsar-kart-sil.

N

Nails (finger)	chath-latch.	20	tsar-kaits.
iron nails	klap-a-koob.	30	kar-hook.
Naked (without clothing)		40	art-leik.
male	sho-she-dáhh.	50	art-lei-kish-kluh.
female	she-she-dä-tartl.	60	wee-ouk-ish.
Name	á-juk-kluk-kik.	70	wee-ouk-ish-kluh.
Near	klar-weich-i-ka.	80	boh-kwe-uk.
Neck	tse-kwar-bits.	90	boh-kwe-uk-ish-kluh.
Needle	kar-juk.	100	sheutch-e-uk.
Nest (bird's)	par-huts.	(Any things round or oval, as pans, cups, plates, eggs, beads, &c., are counted with the following terminals to the simple numbers:—)	
Never	wake-kä-kwows.		
New	soost-ko.		
Night	ut-haie.		
Nine	sar-kwas-sub.		
No	wä-kce or wake-issc.	1	tsark-wark.
None	wake-kade.	2	attl-kuptl.
Noon	takh-assie.	3	wee-á-kuptl.
Nose	choo-oath-tl-tub.	4	boh-kuptl.
Now	kluh-o-ko-wie or kluh.	5	sheutche-a-kuptl.
Numerals[1]		6	cheh-partl-kuptl.
(In counting, it is usual to enumerate ten, and then commence at one, repeating in tens, and at the end of each call the number, thus: ten, kluh; two tens or twenty, tsarkaits; three tens or thirty, karhook, &c.)		7	at-tleph-o-kuptl.
		8	ar-tles-sub-o-kuptl.
		9	sar-kwassub-o-kuptl.
		10	kluh-o-kuptl.
		(Articles having length, as rope, cloth, &c., have the terminal ailsh, which also means fathoms.)	
1	tsark-wark or tsar-kwok.		
2	attl or uttl.	2	attl-ailsh.
3	wee.	3	wee-ailsh.
4	boh.	4	boh-ailsh.
5	sheutche.	5	sheutche-ailsh.
6	cheh-partl.	6	cheh-partl-ailsh.
7	at-tleph or attl-poh.	7	at-tleph-ailsh.
8	ar-tles-sub.	8	ar-tlessub-ailsh.
9	sar-kwás-sub.	9	sar-kwas-sub-ailsh.
10	kluh.	10	kluh-ailsh.

[1] The method of counting on the fingers is as follows: they commence with the little finger of the left hand, closing each finger as it is counted; then pass from the left thumb, which counts five, to the right thumb, which counts six, and so on to the little finger of the right hand, which counts ten. I have sometimes seen Indians commence counting with the little finger of the right hand, but it is invariably the custom to commence with that finger instead of a thumb.

THE INDIANS OF CAPE FLATTERY. 101

Numerals

(In counting fish, or measuring oil or potatoes, they make use of the terminal *ul*, which is an expression of assent. One person will call the number, which another will repeat, adding the terminal *ul*, meaning, as we would say, this is one, this is two, &c.)

1	*tsark-wark.*
2	*attl-ul.*
3	*wee-ul.*
4	*boh-ul.*
5	*sheutche-ul.*
6	*cheh-partl-ul.*
7	*at-tleph-ul.*
8	*ar-tles-sub-ul.*
9	*sar-kwas-sub-ul.*
10	*kluh-ul.*

O

Oar	*e-sáib-e-suk.*
Off shore	*hai-árt-stat.*
Oil	*kár-took.*
Olden time or formerly	*ho-ái-o-kwi.*
Old man	*ai-chope.*
Old woman	*ái-chub.*
On or towards shore	*klar-wárt-stat.*
One	*tsar-kwart* or *tsar-kwoks.*
Open	*kotle-tah.*
Opposite or the other side	*kwis-pairk.*
Otter	*kar-tówe.*
Ours, we, or us	*do-wár-do.*
Outdoors	*uée-á-aiks* or *kwee-á-aiks.*
Out of the canoe	*oós-tah-setl.*
Overturn	*hoke-shitl.*
Owl	*took-te-kwad-die.*
Oyster	*kloh-kloh.*
thorn oyster (*Spondylus*)	*ko-ok'h-sa-aé-buts.*

P

Paddle, *a*	*kla-táh-juk.*
Paddle, *to*	*klé-huk.*
Peas	*tsoosk-shitl.*
Penis	*ché-war.*

People	*kleits-á-kwad-die.*
Pigeon	*háy-aib.*
Pipe	*kúsh-sets.*
Pitch	*kluk-áil-á-bis.*
Plank	*kló-ailth.*
Plants	
barberry	*klook-shitl-ko-bupt.*
berries	*hóats-á-kupt.*
fern	*dil-se-bupt.*
grass	*klar-kupt.*
kamass	*kwad-dis.*
rush	*sal-láh-hutl.*
sallal (*Gualtheria*)	*sal-láh-ha-bupt.*
salmon-berry	*kar-ke-wai.*
salmon-bush	*kar-ke-weep.*
salmon-sprouts	*ko-kose-kárdlth.*
strawberry	*hár-de-tup.*
thumb-berry (*Rubus odoratus*)	*lo-lo-wits.*
sprouts of the same	*kothl-kowie.*
cranberry	*páp-pas.*
red huckleberry	*héy-se-ahd.*
blue huckleberry	*ko-ho-ák-tl.*
gooseberry	*shatch-káh-bupt.*
currant	*ha-pá-pá-bupt.*
crab apple	*dópt-ko-bupt.*
white birch	*klá-hap-partl.*
alder	*kwárk-sah-bupt.*
spruce	*do-hó-bupt.*
hemlock	*klar-kár-bupt.*
cedar	*klá-e-shook.*
yew	*klá-hairk-tle-bupt.*
dogwood	*kitl-che-bupt.*
elder	*sik-ke-ár-she-bupt.*
liverwort	*thle-thle-sús-sok-kowie.*
bittersweet	*bar-chil-loh-kowie.*
liquorice (*Polypodium falcatum*)	*hur-há-tee.*
nettles	*kau-lup-kay.*
blind nettles	*a-dab-a-bupt.*
arbutus uva ursi	*klár-kupt.*
vine evergreen	*tsee-tsee-ess.*
tobacco	*kóo-shá.*
Plenty	*ar-ke-yák.*
Point, *to*	*kope-shitl.*
Point or end	*yu-chil-tish.*
Poor	*há-há-datl.*
very poor, unfortunate	*tlá-kwo.*
Porpoise	*tsáilth-ko.*
Potatoes	*kau-its.*
Poultry	*a-há-há*
cock	*a-há-hácha-kope.*
hen	*a-há-háhai-up.*
Pound, *to*	*kláts-klai.*

102   THE INDIANS OF CAPE FLATTERY.

Pour, *to*	*klook-sáp-gie.*	Return	*ho-wái.*
Powder	*bóot-sis-suk.*	by and by return	*ar-déci-ho-wái.*
Pregnant	*kleet-séet.*	Rifle	*tsoo-tsark-will.*
Presently	*ar-déci.*	Ring, *finger*	*kă-kú-buk-e-dú-kup.*
Prongs of fish-gig	*hèche-ta-kethl-tub.*	River	*tsă-ark.*
Pronouns		Road or trail	*tar-shee.*
I	*seir.*	Roast by the fire	*kla-ah-pis.*
I work	*ohó-bits-kwi-seir.*	Rope	*ses-tópe.*
I laugh	*ohúse-ö-ă-wika.*	Rotten, as wood	*kwer-kwer-juk-tl.*
my	*o-kwiks-te.*	as fruit	*ko-it-ják.*
thou	*sú-er.*	Rum	*lum-muks.*
he	*ohó-te-da.*	Run, *I*	*ă-hárts-its.*
we	*ohode.*	Rush	*sal-lôh-hutl*
ye	*do-bits.*		
they	*ah-dithl-tits.*		
Proud	*to-póh.*		S
I am proud	*to-póots.*		
he is proud	*to-tó-bush.*	Sallal berries	*kár-ke-sup*
they are proud	*tóp-kwitl.*	Salmon	
Pudenda	*jude.*	spring or silver	*tsóo-it.*
Push, *to.*	*chák-shitl.*	young	*tsow-thl.*
		summer	*háh-did.*
	Q	dog-tooth	*cheéch-kowis.*
		trout	*hó-pid.*
Quick; *come quick*	*ut-sai-shoo-oókh.*	Salmon roe	*ách-pahb.*
Quills	*ki-thla-id.*	Salmon berries	*kar-ke-wai.*
		Salt	*too-púthl.*
	R	Salute on meeting a friend	
		to a male	*kwátch-im.*
Rain	*beit-la* or *beitlal.*	to a female	*koáth-lub.*
Rainbow	*tsów-a-ūse.*	Sand	*ses-sá-bits.*
Rake	*kle-pé-ak.*	Sandpiper	*ho-hópe-sis.*
Raven	*klook-shóod.*	Saw	*chec-te-ak.*
Receive, *to*	*tsoo-kwitl.*	Scallop	*bo-whits-ae.*
Red	*klô-hoke.*	Soulpin	*ka-biss.*
Relations	*ó-o-arts.*	Sea (salt water)	*too-páhlcha-uk.*
father	*dó-wiks* or *dó-aks.*	Sea-fowl	*hooke-toop.*
mother	*ă-baiks.*	Sea-lion	*ár-ká-wad-dish.*
grandfather	*da-dairks.*	Seal, hair	*kars-chówe.*
grandmother	*ko-iáks.*	fur	*kaíth-la-doos.*
son, *my* (child)	*a-kúse-ch.*	Seal's bladder	*kal-lá-ka-chub.*
son (grown up)	*ó-sha-hode.*	Seal's paunch	*koo-yow.*
daughter, *my* (child)	*há-dów-e-chuk.*	Seal-skin buoy	*du-koop-kuptl* or *do-ko-kuptl.*
(grown up)	*ă-tuk-hu-áttl-bus.*		
husband, *my*	*chá-kope.*	Seasons	
wife, *my*	*hái-up.*	spring	*klairk-shitl.*
brother, *elder*		summer	*klu-pairtch.*
said by a male	*tak-ke-ai.*	autumn	*kwi-atch.*
said by a female	*hah-chóop-siks.*	winter	*wake-pentl.*
brother, *younger*	*kar-thláil-ik.*	Seat, *the*	*wák-its.*
sister, *elder*	*kloo-chuk-sub.*	See, *to*	*dartl-shitl.*
younger	*bá-bô-ik-sa.*	I see	*ohose-dartl-chatl.*
half-sister	*yu-kwa-uk-sa.*	I do not see	*chár-dis.*

THE INDIANS OF CAPE FLATTERY. 103

See; look; to call the attention	klĕd-ăla.
Seine	ché-iks.
Seven	attleph or attl-poh.
Sew, to	de-kă-dek.
thread	de-káib.
Shadow	ko-ăi-e-chid.
Shark	sah-bass.
Sharp	káck-shitl.
Shells	kai-ish-kud-dy.
Ship	bar-bethld.

(This is a Nootkau word, mar-meth-ld, and signifies a house on the water. It is also applied to all white men, and signifies, when so applied, those who came in or who live in houses on the water.)

Shirt	kle-hairk-tl.
Shoes	klă-klă-kús-tobe.
Short	dé-its.
Shot	klă-klă-to-kwók-ut-shitl.
Shoulder	klă-ho-pa-tie.
Shovel	chat-kard.
Shut or close, to	boo-shă-it-tă.
Shuttleoock	o-kó-ey.
Sick	tă-ithl.
Sing	du-duke.
Sister	
elder	klu-chŭk-sub.
younger	bar-bă-ik'-sa.
Sit, to	klă-dairk.
squat down	klă-deilth.
you sit down	ta-kwit-la-dáit-so or ta-kwitl-suer.
I will sit down	ta-kwit-lik-seir.
all sit	ta-kwilsh.
Six	chrh-partl.
Skate (the fish)	bil-lă-chie.
Skin	klă-hark.
Skunk	ă-ăil-ă-hai-use.
Sky	hac-tah-ártstl.
Slave	ko-thlo.
common person	mis-che-mas or bis-che-bas.
Sleep	wée-atch.
Slow	klă-wá.
when applied to persons	wee-wich-kub-bik.
when applied to ships or canoes	wée-chook.
when applied to animals	wée-chu-kuptl.
Small	kwă-ôw-e-chuk.
Smallpox	he-he-dathl.
Smell, to	bé-shitl.

Smell	
unpleasant smell	u-bus-suk be-shitl.
agreeable smell	chab-bas be-shitl.
Smoke	kóo-sha.
Snake	tlay-ee.
Sneeze, to	too-toóp-uks.
Snow	kóo-sié.
Sorrow	kwă-ŭk-wiks-scuk-iktl.
Speak, to	ó-she-buts.
Spear	beelt-sie.
bird-spear	heich-il-tah.
Spear fish, to	hă-poorp.
Spill	hóke-sah.
Split	hey-sis.
Spoon	chat-káirk.
Spring	klăirk-shitl.
Squirrel	sib-be-lab-be.
Stand, to	klaerk-shitl.
Star	tówie-sub-buts.
Steal, to	kvathl.
to snatch or take a thing forcibly	káp-shitl.
Stone	teh-deh-chooh.
Stone pestle or maul for splitting wood	tă-kó-wă-dă-ăks.
Stop (imperatively)	e-yáhh.
remain	e-yăh-has-sic.
Stop; to finish	hé-artl.
Story	kŭm-itl-kups.
Straight	tar-kárpl.
Stranger	hó-o-war-te-duks.
Strawberries	háh-de-tup.
Strike, to	kok-sap.
Strong	dah-shook.
Stubborn	
male	wáy-a-buktl.
female	wă-áib.
Summer	kloop-pairteh.
Sun	kle-sâ-káirk.
Suppose (if)	kwă-kai.
Surf	sis-sā-káh-dă-kás.
Sweet, or pleasant to taste or smell	chab-bas or cham-mas.
Swim	soo-sóoke.

T

Table	ko-aph.
Table with food	how-athl.
Tail	wăh-huta.
Take, to	suk-witl.
Talk, to	ó-she-buts.
Talk, trifling	hé-he-huy.

Talk	
stop your talk, or you talk foolishly	*uthl-kud.*
Tallow	*hā-biks.*
Taste, *to*	*he-dáouks-tl.*
Tell the truth, you do not lie	*tā-ko-bats-suer.* *wake-iss kā-lúk-tliss.*
Ten	*kluh.*
Testicles	*kar-kó-bits.*
Thanks	*ho-shee-árk-shis.*
That	*teé-dah.*
There	*teit-ser.*
They	*do-dobe.*
Thick	*ár-took* or *utt-he.*
Thin	*wát-chid.*
Thirsty	*cha-éer-hus.*
This	*téc-kah.*
Thou	*suer.*
Thunder	*thleu-kloots.*
Thus, or the same	*kwar-ces-sie.*
very good	*kwar-ces-sar.*
Thread	*de-kábe.*
Three	*oui* or *wee.*
Throw away, *to*	*hésh-tsap.*
Tide, *high*	*tsu-bā-i-chish-chuk.*
Tide, *low*	*klu-show-a-chish-chuk.*
Tie, *to*	*bátl-shitl.*
tie canoe	*batl-sap.*
Tired, weary, or **exhausted**	*tahk-ke-á-you.*
Tobacco	*kush-á.*
smoke	*kush-á.*
Tobacco-pipe	*kush-sets.*
to smoke a pipe	*kush-she-áiks.*
To-day	*kle-sée-ā-kow-ā-ka-dic.*
yesterday	*kláo-cheelth.*
Toes	*tsark-tsárk-itl-sub.*
Together	*do-dó-buks.*
To-morrow	*ár-bei* or *ár-bi.*
To-night	*ut-hái-u.*
Tongue	*lā-kairk.*
Towards shore	*klar-wárt-sat.*
Trade, *to*	*bar-kwátl.*
Trail or **road**	*lár-shee.*
Trap	*kap-páirk.*
Tree	*ah-hahts-ish.*
Trencher or **wooden dish**	*klo-kwaks.*
Trifling (jargon *cultus*)	*wake-isse.*
very trifling	*hoh-háh-datl-wake-isse.*
Trout, *brook*	*klá-klek-tso.*
Trowsers	*kla-ish-ja-kuk.*
True	*klu-klo-oshe-buts.*
Trunk or **chest**	*ā-huy-dookst.*
Turn around	
a kettle	*arts-kwe-dúk-sah.*
a canoe	*hóh-who-al.*
or look here	*ar-tis-kwe-dook.*
Two	*attl* or *uttl.*

U

Under	*há-tá-post-luk.*
Understand	*kúm-ber-tups.*
Unpleasant, or offensive to taste or smell	*u-bús-suk.*
(For instance, the smell of a skunk, snuff, ammonia, pungent spices, carrion, &c.; or the taste of vinegar, spice, anything bitter, &c. Whatever is pleasant to taste or smell is termed *chób-bas* or *chám-mas.*)	
Untie	*klúk-tl-sup.*
Up	*hi-ér-chi-ditl.*
Up, to place anything to take anything up and place it on a table	*he-dás-ho.* *he-dás-pe-tup.*
to place anything from a table on the ground or floor	*oas-tap-a-ter.*
Upright, as to stand up or put up a post	*klár-kishl.*
to drive down a stake perpendicularly	*klar-kisht-sā-ho.*
Upset	*kook-sah.*
Up stream	*há-dárd-tl.*
down stream	*ik-tark-wárk-kliss.*
get up, applied to a child	*sé-kah.*

V

Vinegar	*tse-há-puthl.*

W

Wagon	*tsark-tsárk-as.*
Walk, *to*	*tlā-uk.*
Want, *to*	*o-ote-sus.*
Warm	*kloo-partl.*
Warrior	*wé-e-buktl.*
Wash, *to*, the head	*tso-ai-ouk.*
the face	*tso-kwów-itl.*
the person	*hah-táhd.*
clothes	*tso-kwill-gec.*

Water	*chă-ouk* or *chă-uk.*		Wind	
Waterfall	*toó-wăhl.*		east wind	*too-loóch-ah-kook.*
Waves	*whe-ups.*		west wind	*wa-shĕl-lie.*
Weary; exhausted	*tahk-ke-ŭ-you.*		southeast wind	*boo-chée.*
We	*ohóde.*		northwest wind	*yu-yoke-sis.*
Wedge	*klăr-dit.*		Wings	*klap-ă-hub.*
Weir for fish	*boo-shóo-war.*		Winter	*wake-parthl* or *bot-lăthl.*
Whale (generic)	*chet-a-pook.*		Within or in	
What	*buk-kuk* or *art-juk.*		canoe	*c-lăks-is.*
what do you want	*búk-ke-klair-sik.*		house	*băt-che-ailth.*
what are you doing	*búk-ke-da-har-pik.*		Wolf	*choo-choo-ukstl.*
what is your name	*art-juk-klŭk-ish.*		Woman	*har-dairk.*
what is his name; an			old woman	*ai-chub.*
expression of doubt			Wood, dead	*pathl-hukt.*
when trying to think			Work	*bar-boo-ak.*
of a person's name	*cha-kă-dah.*		Worthless	*pĕ-shak.*
Wheat	*bar-ba-chĕss-kook.*		Wrist	*he-he-diăr-kwe-dook.*
Where	*wa-as.*		Write, to	*char-tar-tle.*
where are you going	*wa-ăs-a-kleesh* or *wa-ăs-a-kartl.*		writing or drawing	*char-tăi-ouks.*
			writer or painter	*chăr-tik.*
where do you come from	*wa-ăs-ă-te-klerk.*			
where do you go	*wa-ăs-a-te-kleesh.*			
Whistle, to	*să-săhb.*		**Y**	
White	*kle-sóok.*			
White men	*bar-bethld.*		Yard, measure	*kart-sark.*
Who	*art-juk.*		Yawn, to	*pas-tăhk-shitl.*
Why	*ba-ka-dah.*		Yes	*a-oh* or *hăh.*
Wife	*hai-up.*		Yesterday	*clă-o-cheelth.*
Wind	*wake-sie.*		You	*suer.*
north wind	*batl-el-tis.*		Young man	*klă-hoke-shĕ-tlăi-sad.*
south wind	*kwart-see-die*		Yours	*su-wătch.*

NOTE.—The following words which appear in the text do not belong to the Makah, but are "Jargon" words, derived from other languages.—G. G.

Cultus, Chinook *kul-tas,* worthless; good for nothing; inferior.

Skookoom, Chihelis *sku-kŭm,* a ghost; an evil spirit or demon.

Tamanawas, Chinook *i-ta-ma-na-was,* a guardian or familiar spirit; magic; luck; fortune; anything supernatural; conjuring.

LOCAL NOMENCLATURE OF THE MAKAH.

Kwe-nait-che-chot. Tribal name.
Dwart or *Deeah.* Neeah Bay and village.
Chardi. Tatoosh Island. This is also termed *Opa-jeeta,* or the island.
Ho-selth. Village at Flattery Rocks.
Tsoo-ess. Village on the Tsooyes River, near its mouth.
Tsów-iss. The rock at the mouth of the river, on its southwest side.

Ba-hó-bo-hosh. The rocky point on the north side of the mouth of the river.
Tsoo-yescha-uk. The river flowing past the Tsooess village.
Wa-atch. Village at mouth of Waătch Creek.
Ar-kŭt-tle-kowcer. Point west of Waătch village.
Kid-de-kŭb-but. A village half-way between Tutoosh Island and Neeah Bay.
Bă-ă-dah. The eastern point of Neeah Bay.

Koit-láh. The western point of Neeah Bay.
Wa-ád-dah. Island between Bä-ä-dah and Koit-láh points.
Sah-da-ped-thl. Rocks west of Kiddekubbut village, on which H. B. M. steamer Hecate struck in 1861 (Aug. 19th).
Kre-sis-so. The rocks at the extreme point of Cape Flattery.
Tsar-tsar-dark. The conspicuous pillar rock at the northwest extremity of Cape Flattery.

To-kwák-sose. A small stream running into the Straits of Fuca, two miles east of Neeah Bay.
Kaithl-ka-ject. Sail rock opposite the mouth of Tokwaksose River.
Sik-ke-u. A river east of the Tokwaksose.
Hó-ko. A river six miles east of the Tokwaksose, a fork of the Sikkeu.

(This river is incorrectly spelled Okĕho. The Makahs strongly aspirate the first syllable, and pronounce as I have written it, *Hó-ko*.)

Klä-klá-wice. Clallam Bay.

INDEX.

Acanthias Suckleyi, 29
Adze, 34
Age of Makahs, 4
Ahchawat, 6
A-ik·h-pet'hl, 30
A'-ka-wad-dish, 30
Anarrhichthys, 30
Arbutus uva ursi, 27
Arrows, 47
Arum, 31
A-tlis-tat, 21
Aurora, 87

Ba-bet'-hl-ká-di, 14
Bah-die, 49
Bark, 18
Bark clothing, 44
Barter for wood, 4
Baskets, 42, 45, 46
Bastard cod, 24, 28
Beds, 5
Berberis, 46
Be-shó-we, 28, 40
Bird-spears, 47, 48
Black skin, 22
Blankets, 32
Boards, 4
Bo-hé-ei, 46
Bo-kwis'-tat, 21
Bows, 47
Boxes, 42
Building, 5

Canoes, 35, 36, 37
Cape Indians, 1
Cha-batta Ha-tartstl, 61
Cha-t'hbuk-dos, 21
Chā-tātl, 7
Cha-tai-uks, 7
Chā-tik, 7, 9, 10
Che-būd, 23
Che-che-wid, 19
Chet'-a-pŭk, 7, 19
Chiefs, 52
Childbirth, 82
Children's amusements, 14
Chisel, 34

Clallam mats, 5
Cleanliness, 19
Cod-hook, 41
Colors, 45
Cooking, 25
Cradle, 18

Dee-aht, 58
Deluge, 57
Diatomaceous earth, 44
Diseases, 79, 80
Disposition of property, 85
Dog-fish oil, 29, 31, 32
Dōpt-kó-kupdl, 21
Do-t'hlub, 62, 75
Dreams, 76
Dress, 15, 16
Drying fish, 7
Duels, 15
Dukwally, 62, 66, 73, 75
Du-pói-ak, 21

Echinus, 24
Eclipses, 90
Esquimaux, 87

Feasts, 26
Feather and dog's hair blankets, 43
Flattening of the head, 3
Fish-club, 42
Fishing-lines, 40
Fish-spears, 47
Food, 19
Forts, 51
Fucus gigantea, 2
Funeral ceremonies, 83

Gambling implements, 44
Games, 44
Gaultheria shallon, 27
Genealogy, 58
Government, 52
Great Spirit, 61

Ha-hék-to-ak, 7, 8, 63
Halibut fishery, 22, 23
Halibut hook, 41
Haliotis, 47
Hammers, 4, 35
Hardiness of Makahs, 4
Harpoons, 19, 20, 39
Hats, 45
He-stuk'-stas, 21
He-sé-yu, 18
He-tuk-wad, 21
Hippo campus, 8
History, 55
Hosett, 6
Houses, 4
Hul-liák, 44
Hul-li-á-ko-bupd, 44

Interior of a lodge, 7

Käb-bis, 28
Ká-dátl, 28
Ka-kaitch, 8
Ka-kai-woks, 21
Kák-te-wahd'-de, 42
Kös-chó-we, 30
Kät-hta-dás, 30
Kaú-wid, 19
Kelp, 40
Kid-de-kub-but, 6
Kla-hap-pák, 28
Klas-ko-kopp'h, 19
Klas-set, 1
Klé-sea-kark-tl, 62
Kle-tait-tish, 21
Kli-cha, 21
Klook-shood, 65
Klüksko, 21
Knives, 34
Kobetsi, 88
Kó-che-tin, 23
Kóts-kŭ, 19
Kwa-kwau-yak'-t'hle, 19
Kwak-watl, 30
Kwahtie, 64
Kwartscedie, 92
Kwe-kapdl, 21

(107)

INDEX.

Kwe-nĕt-sat'h, 1
Kwe-nĕt-chĕ-chal, 1
Kŭt-so-wit, 21

Labrets, 18
Ladles, 26, 27
La-hull, 44
La-hullum, 44

Magic, 76
Makah census, 2
Makah reservation, 1
Makah villages, 6
Mak-kah, 1
Manufactures, 35
Manufacture of canoes, 4
Marriage, 11, 13
Marriageable age, 12
Masks, 69
Mats, 42, 45
Medicine, 76, 78
Mink, 64
Mixed blood among Makahs, 3
Months, 91
Moxas, 79
Mussels, 24
Mythology, 61

Natica, 81
Neeah, 6
Neeah Bay, agriculture at, 2
Neeah Bay, animals at, 2
Neeah Bay, climate at, 2
Neeah Bay, soil at, 2
Nose ornaments, 17
Neshwâts, 8

Octopus tuberculatus, 23
Onychotenthis, 24
Origin, 56
Ornaments, 45, 47
Otter, 27
Oysters, 24

Pa-dan-t'hl, 21
Paddles, 37
Paint, 17

Painting, 9, 10
Parapholas, 89
Pĕ-ko, 46
Physical characteristics of Makahs, 3
Picture writing, 7
Pillar rock, 86
Pipe clay, 44
Polypodium falcatum, 80
Polygamy, 13
Porpoises, 30
Potatoes, 23, 25
Pot-lat-ches, 13
Pottery, 48
Punishments, 53
Pyrola elliptica, 79

Rainbows, 90
Rattles, 77
Raven, 65
Roofs, 6
Ropes, 39
Rubus odoratus, 25
Rubus spectabilis, 25, 27

Scallops, 24
Scilla esculenta, 25
Seals, 30
Seal-skin buoy, 20
Sea-otter, 30
Seasons, 91
Seclusion of girls, 12
Se-hwau, 19
Se-kā-jĕe-ta, 87
Shamanism, 76
Shogh, 5
Skoo-koom, 63
Slaves, 10
Smoking, 27
Sneezing, 61
Social life, 10
Songs, 49
South wind, 92
Spanish settlement, 55
Spears, 47
Spoons, 26
Squid, 24
Stature of Makahs, 3
Stone weapons, 49
Superstitions, 86

Tamanáwas ceremonies, 9, 13, 61
Tatooche Island, 1, 6, 60
Tattooing, 18
Te-ka-aŭ-da, 21
Thlu-klŭts, 7, 8, 72
Thorn-oyster, 79
Thunder-bird, 7, 9
Tides, 66
Ti-juk, 30
Time, 91
Ti-ne-t'hl, 23
Tools, 33
Toosh-kow, 28, 90
Trade, 30, 31
Traditions, 55
Treatment of women, 11
Treaty of 1855, 1
Tsa-bâ-hwa, 28
Tsá-daitch, 28
Tsailt'h-ko, 30
Tsa-kwat, 21
Tsiárk, 62, 72, 75
Tsis-ka-pul, 21
Tsuess, 6
Tŭsh-kaú, 28, 90
Tu-tŭtsh, 8
Twins, 82

U-butsk, 21

Vocabularies, 93

Wäntch, 6
Wäatch Creek, 2
Wäntch Marsh, 2
Warfare, 50
Whales, 7, 19
Whale oil, 22
Whales' bones, 8
Whaling, 19
Whaling canoe, 21
Whaling gear, 39
Wooden utensils, 42, 43
Wrestling, 15

Ya-cha, 29
Yakh'yu-bad-die, 19

PUBLISHED BY THE SMITHSONIAN INSTITUTION

WASHINGTON CITY,

MARCH, 1870.

www.ingramcontent.com/pod-product-compliance
Lightning Source LLC
Chambersburg PA
CBHW031400160426
43196CB00007B/831